*To Blake*
*It was truly a pleasure meeting you and your wife*

# EYES CLOSED, TOO HEAR

### RJ Woodward

*RJ Woodward*

Box 1046
Kamsack, SK
S0A 1S0

iUniverse, Inc.
New York   Bloomington

# Eyes Closed, Too Hear

*Copyright © 2010 RJ Woodward*

*All rights reserved. No part of this book may be used or reproduced by any means, graphic, electronic, or mechanical, including photocopying, recording, taping or by any information storage retrieval system without the written permission of the publisher except in the case of brief quotations embodied in critical articles and reviews.*

*iUniverse books may be ordered through booksellers or by contacting:*

*iUniverse*
*1663 Liberty Drive*
*Bloomington, IN 47403*
*www.iuniverse.com*
*1-800-Authors (1-800-288-4677)*

*Because of the dynamic nature of the Internet, any Web addresses or links contained in this book may have changed since publication and may no longer be valid. The views expressed in this work are solely those of the author and do not necessarily reflect the views of the publisher, and the publisher hereby disclaims any responsibility for them.*

*ISBN: 978-1-4502-6197-5 (pbk)*
*ISBN: 978-1-4502-6198-2 (ebk)*

*Printed in the United States of America*

*iUniverse rev. date: 10/20/10*

# **Contents**

Prologue ........................................................................... ix
1. In the Beginning ........................................................ 1
2. Destiny ....................................................................... 7
3. Purpose .................................................................... 19
4. The End .................................................................... 24
5. Romance .................................................................. 34
6. Heritage ................................................................... 39
7. Hidden Facts ........................................................... 43
8. To Judge .................................................................. 48
9. Pets .......................................................................... 52
10. Military .................................................................... 56
11. Cremation ................................................................ 60
12. Faults ....................................................................... 64
13. Money Effects ......................................................... 72
14. Momentous Events ................................................. 77
15. Epiphanies ............................................................... 81
16. Kids in the Hood ..................................................... 86
17. Keepsakes ................................................................ 94
18. Horoscopes .............................................................. 99
19. Unconditional Love ............................................... 103
20. The Draw ............................................................... 106
21. Tattoos ................................................................... 109
22. Images ................................................................... 112

23. The Truth ..................................................................... 117
24. Auras ........................................................................... 120
25. Our Choices ................................................................ 123
26. The Butler ................................................................... 127
27. Procrastination ........................................................... 130
28. Meditation .................................................................. 134
29. Christmas pudding ..................................................... 137
30. Dreams ....................................................................... 140
31. Humble ....................................................................... 146
32. Comfort foods ............................................................ 149
33. Lotteries ..................................................................... 152
34. Poems ........................................................................ 156
35. Quotes ....................................................................... 160
36. Politically Correct ....................................................... 163
37. Flowers ...................................................................... 166
38. The Dance .................................................................. 170
39. Carpentry ................................................................... 173
40. Words Ending in "tion" ............................................... 176
41. The Cabin ................................................................... 181
42. Bears .......................................................................... 186
43. Travels ....................................................................... 188
44. Negativity ................................................................... 192
45. Argument ................................................................... 195
46. Humour ...................................................................... 197
47. Joy .............................................................................. 202
48. The Daunted ............................................................... 204

| | | |
|---|---|---|
| 49. | Rational | 207 |
| 50. | Parables | 209 |
| 51. | One's Grief | 212 |
| 52. | Share Your Story | 219 |
| 53. | Too Heal | 223 |
| 54. | Then Sings My Soul | 226 |
| 55. | A Gift | 230 |
| 56. | My Angels | 233 |
| 57. | Repent | 236 |
| 58. | In the Garden | 238 |
| 59. | Amazing Grace | 242 |
| 60. | Real Deal | 245 |
| 61. | Mysteries | 248 |
| 62. | I Love You | 251 |
| 63. | The Seed | 254 |

# **Prologue**

I have always wanted to write a book. I felt it was in my destiny and my initial thoughts were it would have something to do with Family History. I have been doing Family Research for forty some years now and my family tree has gotten so big that to write a book about it would be never-ending and pointless. I am now realizing a whole different purpose to where this research is taking me. So let's get started.

    I have never felt I was truly in control of my life. A broad statement, but true, I have always felt I was being guided to an ultimate purpose. Even as a child, my interests weren't heavy sports related, my friends were limited by my own selection and I was driven to different undertakings such as Taxidermy, Genealogy and Numerology.

    My mother raised us with a strong discipline of religion and I always believed she was hoping to raise the perfect family but as my depths of family history expanded. It was in her blood. Her family tree branched through a long line of strong-minded deacons and reverends. Some would say; heavy duty evangelists. I have come to the belief that, these trails weaving back and forth, here and there throughout our family history are all for a purpose. Each seed planted is to form us to the ultimate being ready to receive our final reward at the end of time.

One point, I have come to realize, we interconnect with like thinking people at key times in our lives. We believe these people will remain as friends till the end of time, but they don't. Why!! We have messages to pass on, either through actions or support and then we move on. Our chance meeting again, depends on the directions we have to follow. Now some are going to say this is really deep, but it isn't. It is really quite simple and you will see this as we go along.

There are no coincidences in life, every action or situation is for a reason. This story is a compiling of stories with no beginning or end rather a snapshot in time.

> *"Thou shalt not be a victim. Thou shalt not be a perpetrator. Above all, thou shalt not be a bystander" - Holocaust Museum, DC*
>
> *"When you have once seen the glow of happiness on the face of a beloved person, you know that a man can have no vocation but to awaken that light on the faces surrounding him; and you are torn by the thought of the unhappiness and night you cast, by the mere fact of living, in the hearts you encounter."*
> *Albert Camus*
>
> *"Your work is to discover your work, and then with all your heart give yourself to it..."*
> *Gautama Siddharta, the founder of Buddhism, 563-483 BC*

Being openhearted means tapping into the social connectedness that lies at the core of the human experience and recognizing that it is through genuine feelings of appreciation for other people that we derive our strength, balance and stability. When I practice openheartedness, I can come to a place where I can let go of the things that trouble me and open myself up.

This book is dedicated to the ones with their hearts open willing to receive a heavenly gift. With the seed of faith planted for generations to come.

> *"You must be the change you wish to see in the world." ~ Mahatma Gandhi*

> *"Freedom is what you do with what's been done to you." - Jean-Paul Sartre*

> *"The people who are lifting the world onward and upward are those who encourage more than they criticize." ~ Elizabeth Harrison*

## Chapter One

# In the Beginning

One would think starting with "Once Upon A Time" would work, but in this case "NO". My direction seems to be a life story, with direction, a moulding of human life that could pertain to anyone.

I was born just after the end of World War II, to young parents struggling to survive. My father was the son of a baker. A son for who was given a two wheeled-bike with wooden wheels; not for pleasure; rather to deliver bread every day after school. He like his brothers, were never afforded the opportunity to achieve a full education, rather to enter the family business after completing Grade 8. Knowing the Family business was all they needed, as like many young men during this time jumped at the chance to leave home at the first chance. This being WW II, lying about his age he entered the Canadian Navy at the age of 15. Dad and his older brother parted ways in Winnipeg one going in the Navy the other in the Army. Not knowing at that time only one would return. Serving his time, he returned home and helped his oldest brother work his bakery. My mother was working in the Bake Shop at this time and needless to say the rest is history. They got married and I was born.

My father never got the love of military life out of his system, he re-enlisted in the Canadian Army because he felt it would be a more stable life with a family. My grandfather on hearing this met up with dad in Winnipeg and enticed him to return home to run his business and a promise of a home of his own to raise the family. Dad regretted this decision till the day he died. After my grandfather's death, dad worked alongside his mother in the bakery for several more years. Times were changing, the bakery needed modernization and my grandmother took the stand it was good enough for your father it is good enough for you. Dad left, the bond between mother and son were never the same up until the day she passed. Dad bounced between jobs trying to find his nitch. Then one day by chance, a friend of the family who owned a Plumbing and Heating Shop, happened to ask if dad could do a few hours work. He remained there till he retired. The owner of the shop was killed in an airplane crash and dad became a co-owner along with other members of the staff.

My Dad's father, came from England, he was the oldest child from parents that died; within months of each; of consumption. There has always been a discussion over the prior lineage a grey area that has been lost or buried in tattered records waiting for someone to find. He was in his teens, restless and left to spend several years in the merchant marines. My Dad's mother's parents, being in partnership, with my Great grandparents took the remaining children and raised them as their own. This blended family moved to Canada. My grandmother's family setup a homestead in the newly developing west. Grand-dad followed, where my Grandparents were later married.

These were hard times and the family moved from job to job, all bakeries until my grandfather settled down with his own family business. He liked his beverage and I remember the old ginger beer bottles like it was yesterday. There is a banner in the United Church that he tried to paint after a few rums, the story goes the paint ran down the wall faster than he could move the brush and he humbly had to fix it all before the next Sunday's services.

In his own way, he had a heart of gold. As kids we would go to visit in our Sunday best and Grand-dad would give each of us the stickiest chocolate candy just to see the mess we could get in. My second oldest sister had red hair, his favourite, because her hair matched his cherished Irish Setters. When I got my first pair of good pants, he gave me a silver dollar to fill the pocket.

Its these little things that stick in the mind and keep coming back generations later. It was always said that during the war, the poor and needy always came to his bakery for day old leftovers as if there was a special mark on the front of his store guiding them in for a bite to eat.

Dad came from a family of nine brothers and sisters; they were all encouraged (strongly) to be in the local church choir directed by my grandfather. Singing and music was a key part of the family upbringing and every family member had stories that would curl your hair relating to the firm direction used to implant this fatherly virtue in his children. Grand dad was singing in a boys' choir in a cathedral when he was the age of five. This carried on through the rest of his life.

Dad was not raised directly by his mother. He was raised by his "Auntie" a live-in nurse, who guided the younger children while my Grandmother maintained the front-end or retail aspect of the bakery. Each girl in the family had the aspiring task to work this area as they grew up. My two older sisters often remark where I was the older male child, the continuance of the family name. I received privileges they could only dream of. I often was served an old English steak and kidney pie where they had a bowl of long cooked heavy porridge. They both remember gagging on every spoonful.

When Dad's mother died, her house was cleaned out. I mean cleaned out, any family history was destroyed, to a budding Genealogist a sin beyond all sins. I was too young to have an input. The years I spent trying to rebuild that history is beyond belief. There are traces left and someday I will gain access to the remaining pieces of this jig-saw puzzle.

The Nurse "Auntie" remained in the family home until it was her time to go. Dad would visit her at least once a week. She would give him a "White Owl" cigar to smoke while he was there. He always had to leave the butt in the ashtray; it was her way in feeling the presence of someone else in the house. On the next visit the ashtray was cleaned and the ritual started all over. Anybody remembering her, and that is a quickly disappearing number, remember her stern English accent announcing "Visiting Hours Are Over" in our local hospital. And that meant they were over, period. No questions asked. On her death, she was cremated and her ashes were spread over the valley she so loved. No marker to show she ever existed, a sore spot with me to this day.

The reason I am laying out these earlier years is they all mould my life to this day. We do not realize in our early years how much influence each and every day to day action has to guide us along our path of life. We are the by product of each of these influences.

My mother's father worked as a station agent for the Canadian National Railway. He was raised in Nova Scotia, where his mother had a very religious input into his life. I say his with tongue in cheek because she was almost to the point of being a strong evangelistic disciple. My Grandfather's dad left to find work in the West and he too worked for the CNR, many attempts were made to move the family West, but Great Gran would have no part of it.

Her direction was to bring religion and faith to the troops going to war. My mother often remarks how as a child she had to brush her grandmother's hair for hours with not so much as a thank you. On the contrary, there was more apt to be a complaint over how it was carried out.

Mom was the oldest child in her family, raised to be perfect in the eyes of the Lord. Now like so many forced to follow that upbringing, you tend to lean towards other interests and she married my dad at 16. Thus leaving, one family and moving in with a larger one to start her own. Like any marriage when you take two different individuals from two different walks of life. Two different upbringings there are many challenges you have to work through and blend. They did that successfully for sixty years, till Dad's passing.

Mom's mother was always prim and proper. She was an angel in her own right and did everything in her power to make a life for her family. She became very forth right in her old age and selected her time to leave this earth in peace and contentment. She left as graceful as she lived her life. In all adversities she usually bit her tongue and lived her life knowing the truths she held in her heart would win out in the end. And they did.

My Grandfather went out, fighting every inch of the way. Being ever so present in his seven month fight to leave this earth only proved to be me, his religious beliefs were wrong. Forgiveness was not a way of life for him. His bitter tongue spewed, religious drawl to the end a true pity for anyone that tried to achieve a final closure and a positive memory.

I have some very fond memories of my mother's parents. I spent many a weekend with them in their later years. My uncle and I made a special trip East to move them nearer to the family in the West. I lived closest to them out of all the family so was at their beckoning call. To me this was an honour, I was willing to accept without question. On my grandfather's 80$^{th}$ birthday, I arrived on the scene with a large bottle of bubbly and a bunch of plastic wine glasses. Well all the Do-gooders were mortified because I brought alcohol into my grandparents place until I poured the drink, gave him a glass and made a toast. You couldn't fill those glasses fast enough.

I was never phony with them; if we were having a drink I poured them one also. It was never harsh and it was never left behind. Was I right or wrong I don't know? Life is what you make of it.

> *"What would you attempt to do if you knew you could not fail?"- Robert Shuller.*

## Chapter Two

# Destiny

With the background set, enter my walk down the garden path. I have always felt my destiny is laid out for me. I experience Déjà-Vu on a regular basis to the point of being scary. I have made statements at different times in my life that have turned heads at the time until I realize what has actually happened to myself. My older sister and I have always been on the same wavelength, we can almost complete each other's thoughts at any given time. We are two completely different individuals under two completely opposing purposes in life, yet like thoughts guide us.

My life has always, and I mean always been directed to help others around me. I do this to a fault, I put everyone's interests in front of my own and this is now coming back to haunt me. As a small child, I would get so upset when friends or cousins would come over to play. They would always break the few toys I treasured, to leave me with nothing. So I would fix, repair and shape them into something that would amuse me. I can't say I ever wanted for more, my imagination and determination gave me the skills to make a simplified version of the toy I wanted. To this day I find it extremely hard to ask for anything, I usually go out and get what I need on my own. The thought of rejection always looms in the back of my mind, so it is easier not to ask in the first place.

With toys sometimes it wasn't the kids that got to play with them first. One year, I would like to say I was about six or seven, my two uncles and father played with my Christmas present over the whole holiday. It was my electric train, they had put more miles around those tracks before I even got to turn on the switch. Looking back at it now I am sure glad they weren't playing with my sister's doll house. That Christmas was celebrated at my mother's parents' place which was a small town train station. We also received a game of "Ring Toss" which the parents took great pleasure in playing in the station's freight shed while they partook in a modified punch. They never realized how loud that game got as they played on.

I remember my sister had invited all these kids to her birthday party, my mother said "Where will we sit everyone". I took all the money from my piggy bank and went down town and bought a set of TV trays (the latest thing at that time) and hauled them home. They were bigger than me at that time, but quite a sight going down the street. Another time, Mom wanted a doorbell, again too young to know better I raided the piggy bank and bought her the actual buzzer not realizing there was a whole system that had to go with it. The point being, I was compelled to help once I realized the need.

My mother's dad couldn't boil a pot of water if he wanted to. It was not a requirement in his life, yet I could cook a full course meal by the age of seven. Both my parents worked the bakery then so I learned. They were not all gourmet delights but they were meals. Back then, I had a thing for these allspice cookies, well if one teaspoon was what the recipe called for, and then two had to taste better... Mind you to this day, I will look at a recipe and modify it to my taste without hesitation. Exact measurements still remains only a guideline and my youngest sister measures everything right down to the precise grain. Different needs different directions.

Mentioning my youngest sister, I have five younger sisters and I left home before the youngest one was born. Education was never my strong point, I knew what it took to pass and I strived for that goal. Anyway, my last year of school had me thinking in a whole different direction. My mother was expecting my youngest sister, the house was small, and so I knew it was time. I joined the Navy prior to the end of the school year. My homeroom teacher said to me "Congratulations You will be sitting in the same desk next year" and my quick rebuttal was "Not in this lifetime, I am already in the military". I was enlisted four days after my seventeenth birthday. The need to finish my education became very apparent after a couple years in the military and that mission was accomplished in my spare time.

I don't want anyone to believe for one second that I was a goodie-goodie, I wasn't. Every one of my sisters had to pay for my schoolroom pranks, through every year of their educations. To this day, we still enjoy swapping schoolday tales and my mother just shakes her head. Our latest generations, pull off capers today and we can only shake our heads and call them amateurs. I knew the old schoolhouse discipline and can honestly say experienced it first hand on several occasions. No matter what punishment I received in school, the same was there to meet me when I got home. At least, when receiving the strap in school, there was always the challenge of slipping your hand away quick enough for the Inflictor to strap their own hand. Inevitably this only guaranteed a couple more.. Slow learner, but fun. We had an oak handle clothes brush that mom used to legislate her discipline. It hurt no ifs ands or buts. One day, dad walked in the brush was on the counter and he smacked mom's butt with it, that was the last time we ever seen it. It must have hurt, if you get the drift. We knew it did.

One day my older sister and myself were playing in the back yard. It was early spring the garden was one big mud pit. Kids are as kids do we walked in the garden to test our rubber boots. Sinking very quickly, we stepped out of them because they wouldn't budge. Running in the house to tell mom we lost our boots. Long story short, we didn't get to wear our boots for the rest of that day because mud to the knees on her freshly cleaned floors was not a combination you really wanted to mix.

Once again, I will state each and every one of these actions has brought me to where I am today. I can honestly say I don't hate anyone. I can be mad or disappointed with a person for a short period of time, once I let it go, I forgive them, and life goes on. I believe the problem they created or the life they choose is their path to follow and the consequences are theirs and theirs alone. A firm believer in "We Reap, What We Sow". I have witnessed the end result too many times to not believe. The more you treat a person badly, the problems in your life seem to intensify and spin out of control. So I say don't like to get caught up in it in the first place. I have always told my kids, treat everyone, the way you would like to be treated. Pure and simple, but hard to comply with when you have to be right all the time. Being a Leo and by virtue of this birth-sign, I have taken a long time to get to the point, to practice what I preach. Don't get me wrong, if I see something wrong I will walk the mile to correct it.

We all experience pain at one time or other in our life. So it is said death always happens in threes. In 1992, we must have been behind in our quota, because that was the year to mark all years. Every time we turned around there was another family member gone. That was the year we had our first family reunion, little did we known, it was also a time to say "Good-Bye" to many of the old guard.

My first wife never made it to the family reunion, she died two months later. Cancer is a cruel disease and a person has to wonder, what message can be taken from the pains endured. She went through five years of suffering and we went through five years of pure raw emotions. A person might say "Well, Lots of people have to deal with this on a day to day basis" Very True. The only saving grace was we knew the end was coming. During that period of time, my job placed me together with two other individuals; un-be-known to me at the time the three of us were to walk the same mile. The same mile but in different directions, we all lost our wives. Why... were we brought together for that particular period of time? I was the youngest team member in our group and contrary to traditions was sent on behalf of our team to extend our condolences. I have often questioned "Why Me?" and the same conclusion comes back, this is something you need to learn. To me, this is preparation for something yet to come.

My mother's younger sister came to visit my first wife a short time before she died. My uncle and I witnessed a conversation that had us both leave the room and question each other over what we had heard. They both were talking that they would meet together shortly on the other side and walk through their garden together. The hair actually stood up on the back of my neck over the conversation. Little did we know at the time that they would both be gone within a month of each other. My mother's mother followed a month after that.

I got away ahead of myself and that is my life, I bounce from thought to thought as if they are only seconds apart. Early in my military career, a good friend of mine died in an airplane crash. The day before, I had said to him "Pay attention to what you are doing or it's going to kill you". He laughed and said "If that happens, I'll come back and tell you". The next day he died and his presence was felt. I will leave that there.

A similar situation, but yet quite different, my uncle and family came to visit us in Nova Scotia as they were leaving and we were saying our goodbyes. I said "Good Bye, this is the last time I'll be seeing you!!" That fall, he was killed in a freak hunting accident. Again "Why Me!!" that is where I started to believe we are all here to assist people at predestined periods of our lives.

This will be my last example on this topic. I had a friend in Nova Scotia that as a pastime would go raid lobster traps. I felt this behaviour would be his demise and told him that would be the end of him. And it was, they found his frozen body on the shore next to his capsized boat. The Search and Rescue helicopter brought his lifeless body back. I was working and met the flight. A RCMP officer pushed his body on to the lowered ramp with his foot. That was the closest time I came to running over an ignorant heartless person. I know this person will have received his just reward or is getting to the top of the list to experience it.

The old adage, we can count our true friends on one hand is so very true. We have people moving in and out of our lives at any given time. They may stay for years or just days. Their presence is felt, dialogue exchanged, that may or may not have any apparent reasoning until years later. A dialogue that was meant to happen.. believe it... accept it.

I went with this girl when I first went to Halifax, we drifted apart and our lives went in different directions. For sake of timing, I will say fifteen years later, halfway across the country, we meet again. This time she is a friend of my first wife. One night sitting outside at our picnic table, she asked "Why did we never hit it off" I explained my take on the whole experience. A couple months later, this person and her family moved on. What was the purpose of our chance meeting? Was this meant as closure, so that she could complete her walk through life? We don't always get the answers, even though the experience was lived. I have countless examples that flash through my mind.

I went with another girl just before I went with my first wife. We parted ways. I was researching the celebrations of the 100th Anniversary for the Canadian Navy and by chance hit on a name of an old friend. I emailed him, he responded and one of his questions was "What happened to that child you had in Nova Scotia?" Wham, What Child? Was the immediate response. Long story short, there is a belief that I fathered another child that I didn't know a thing about. Why after forty- some years would I be confronted with this? Is there a message? Am I supposed to find this person? There is a million questions and no answers. I believe if I am needed, this matter will materialize further because I am now aware. Where I pray for forgiveness everyday now, Is this an indicator of what my prayers have revealed? I know there are people on earth that are our guardian angels and on the same note I believe we are here to be other people's guardian angel. Our motivation or inspiration is revealed as the need through unconscious thought or prayer is transmitted.

I believe there are people that walk this earth, that haven't felt these feelings and will go the rest of their lives not experiencing anything more than their selflessness. These type of people will never have a final destiny, I feel for them, but their ignorance and lack of acceptance is their vice. Sorry, it's time to open your heart, plant the seed and grow. There are people that say "Today's churches are money grabbing adventures" I agree and say "Your Church is in Your Heart, It starts there, It ends there, You get out what you put in". It's that simple. To err is human, to forgive is divine well I can vouch for that.

I will take this one step further and just a little deeper. In my family research, I noticed the movement of various family names in and out of the tree. Each of these families introduces their influence into the generations to come and I believe these traces are genetically woven into our make-up. When we meet people, complete strangers sometimes, these sensors recognize the common connection to the past and we exchange our thoughts. I have a quality, to use a term loosely; I look at a person's eyes when we first meet. I can tell their character right off and proceed on that first impression. The eyes to me tell the story, fear, anger, scared, joy or hurt the list is long. To me the eyes lead to the inner soul, their expressions can't be masked. To view eyes that maybe hidden for a brief moment by the wearing of dark glasses.

I now, start each day and end each day with a little prayer. Nothing heavy, just a quick thought to the start and end the day. I give thanks for the day. I ask that my family be taken into the arms of God and their hearts be opened to the teachings of Jesus. I ask for my heart to be open, forgiveness or any errors I have made and to be guided to my final destiny. Nine chances out of ten, a person's image will come to mind and I believe that is someone that needs a special thought. I find the older I get the more focused I get. Maybe this is part of the reason I feel my services are available to those who ask. I don't forgive because I'm weak, I forgive because I'm smart enough to realise people make mistakes.

My second wife is somewhat of a Non-believer, hence the problem. When my youngest son was born, the doctor placed him in my arms. I went for a walk down the dark quiet halls of the hospital, while he cleaned her up. I talked to my son, his little eyes stared up at me and I promised I would be there for him and gently put the sign of a cross on his forehead. I knew having him baptised at an early age would be out of the question, but my gesture was ours alone. There will be a day he will come to his own decision and I pray my influence will bear fruit. He has always had the most gentle heart and believe that speaking on his behalf at birth, planted that seed.

My walk along the path of numerology has identified another level of logic, I never thought I would see. As it is laid out, we select to come back from another life to complete our cycle of Life. Our names and date of birth detail the areas we want to improve on. Looking at my readout has for a simplified translation "Just Blown Me Away" It details my life completely. I have an inner circle that a selected few get to cross. This safeguard keeps be safe, from the people who I don't have complete trust. To gain trust into this area is a sanction, meant for the pure of heart. I am to go through a great transformation and evolve into the person I am meant to be. Personal possessions will have no meaning and I have noticed through the last few months. Mind you when, my first wife was dying, I felt the same pull. Was this an indicator of things to come? Do we know our future without seeing it?

I know through these sensations of Déjà Vu, that I have already walked this mile and can almost relate what is going to happen next. I also know the feeling that passes through me at the time. Beyond words. Are these seeds planted from previous generations implanted in our hearts to correct some error from days gone by or mere messages to move us along our path? Is it like saying you did this the last time and it didn't work why are you doing it again? Whatever the answer, "Been there done that fits!!".

I have waken from a deep sleep to feel I wasn't the only person in the room, turning on the lights to confirm my thought or walking through a dark house to see if there is any movement. These are all eerie thoughts, but at the time so real. I have sensed other family member's needs and usually a follow-up call verifies the need to talk. I believe we all have the quality to relate to situations that have influenced our lives. We can be watching a movie or reading a book when a series of events move us in a strange way or bring a tear out of nowhere. These are seeds from the past, planted to stimulate our senses. We just have to learn to read them and not to fear the outcome.

I have had two uncles on my father's side for one reason or other took their own lives, their lives cut short because if for no other reason than they were experiencing one of their rock bottom moments. They hit a point in their lives that to proceed further was harder to deal with rather than looking inward to deal with the problem in the first place. Once I realized to head deeper into life, the heart had to be open, the barrier before stopping from moving me ahead was lifted and my life took on a whole different purpose.

An experience that was so profound it will stay with me for the rest of my life. This experience was the seed that inspired me to share the sensation to all who cared to follow. If and when you are ever in caught in a position like you feel you are sinking to a depth lower than a snake's belly. Remember to look within, ask for forgiveness for all the mistakes you have made in your life and ask to have your heart opened to the heavenly teachings. A truly repentant heart will experience this revitalization. To regress only puts one in line for further depressions.

Each day offers another series of events that lately have been so profound one has to wonder what is really happening. I have had chance meetings with people that for no apparent reason have inquired into past family history. Is it that I am more acute to these types of encounters or is it the way of the times either way I find it very fascinating?

## The Seeds

*The seeds planted in us,*
*From once our life began.*
*Can only start to grow,*
*When exposed to an open heart.*
*To sprout from the very start,*
*To thrive from one's guiding love,*
*Is like a fast fleeing dove*
*Flying to the heavens' far above.*
*Our seeds within us planted*
*Carry within all the hope.*
*That they will multiply and flourish*
*In a mankind so blessedly nourished.*
*In God's love for eternity.*

*Author – me*


*"You don't design your own life plan; chances are you'll fall into someone else's plan. And guess what they may have planned for you? Not much." -Jim Rohn*

CHAPTER THREE

# Purpose

I have been in numerous situations, that for no other reason than the hand of God has saved me. It wasn't my time or I haven't completed my destiny. Any way you interpret it, I don't know why I am still alive.

As a young teenager, My cousin, best friend and myself were given the task to feed the cattle on my uncle's farm. It was an extremely cold winter's day. We took the team of horses out and hitched them to a sleigh and off we went, did our chores and headed back to the farmyard. The horses knew they were going back to the warm barn; they took off at full gallop. My cousin put his foot on the front support of the sleigh and it broke. My friend on seeing this, and the narrow gateway was looming ahead he jumped off. My cousin fell through the front of the sleigh. There was a sharp right turn leading up to the front of the barn. The sleigh spun out, I dropped flat on the base and held on, the sleigh slid under a hayrack sitting in front of the barn. I remember it went dark, then light and everything stopped. My uncle and other cousin watching the whole procedure from the window came running expecting to pick a life-less body from the sleigh, when I got up and brushed myself off. The other two were the injured ones.

Another time, when I was in the military, I was on a training flight over Maine. I went to sleep in the back of the aircraft and the two young pilots thought they would play a joke on me. They announced over the internal radio "Mayday, Mayday" I jumped up grabbed a parachute in one hand and went to jump out the door. Needless to say there was a couple seconds of pure panic to stop me from completing my evacuation.

Once during my first marriage, we had bought a new fridge so we decided to move the old one into the basement as a beer fridge. I get it to the top of the steps and tell my wife I will tip the fridge and you guide it down the steps. We start down my foot gets stuck between the step and the fridge because she decides to push the fridge to get it moving faster. I slip and the fridge rides up my legs and it rides me all the way down the stairs when I get to the bottom I brace myself and push back so it won't crack my ribs. Meanwhile my wife thinking she just killed me shuts the basement door so she doesn't have to witness the splatter. We laughed about that story every time it was told.

Each generation has their own claim to fame. My youngest son and his friend had a bonfire in the fire pit in the backyard. For some unknown reason other than they wanted to see what would happen if they threw a paint spray can into the fire. The paint can exploded, destroying the fire pit and for the sake of all and mighty they walked away untouched. The explosion sounded like the whole back of the house came off. A lesson learned without dire consequences. Do you think a seed was planted?

We all do things that are beyond stupid. We all take chances. The examples are endless. I know I have done my fair share. As a young teen, I ate an earthworm to impress a girl. Here we are fifty years later and that story will inevitably come out when we start swapping stories with the newer generations. Turn on any nature show and you can see natives eating bugs or insects but I ate an earthworm to impress a girl. It was me, someone they can relate to.

If you really looked at it, we all probably ate mud pies in a sandbox, at a younger age playing house. Each story we relate or pass on establishes a natural bond we seek with our supposed followers. Some time ago, I had the opportunity to go to my dad's sister's 50th anniversary party. When I was a baby, she had a devastating ordeal changing one of my "crappy nappies". You can probably see where this is going, I took a disposable diaper and filled it full of mustard and presented it to her. It broke the ice and we had a real party!! These are the finer moments in life. If no one is hurt and it leaves a lasting memory, we have planted a seed in the hearts of future generations.

I have a cousin that at any special gathering, at one point or other she would appear dressed as Charlie Chaplin. She was not the first to do this, it was a stunt carried out by our Great Aunt Nan. The seed was planted and bore fruit to re-appear in another generation. If this gesture is to carry on another generation it will appear again performed by a inspired family member. This cousin at her first wedding, I went in my white naval uniform, the party got quite intense another cousin wanted to try on my uniform and I ended up wearing a rhubarb leaf. Not the most impressing site at the time but a story that has lasted four generations. Another time, whereby the "Grace of God", I got home. Just as an antidote, this glowing couple had a Volkswagen, of which we carried into the barn and turned it sideways in a stall. That was probably the initial step to the demise of that marriage.

I remarked about Déjà-vu earlier, I have a nephew another Leo. That is walking virtually parallel to me, a good many years apart. I marvel at the similarities. If we could only combine initiatives to master our destinies but I know that is absolutely impossible. We have the planted seed in us, but also have the challenge in how we are going to deal with it to get to our final destiny. He hasn't had the inspiration to write a book yet, so maybe he gets to do another alternate ending!

We all have relatives that never touch our lives, some we know, and others that appear with research such as I do in genealogy. Is it our loss or is there a whole different meaning? I would like to think it is the later, that they had to go in a different direction to achieve their ultimate destiny. If their seeds are set to nurture like ours, the end result is working in another sphere. In the old days families intertwined in communities for generations and you can track the results. Now with any part of the world only hours apart, these spheres have taken on wider circles and cultures to intertwine into our influences.

I recently met a person, my car salesman who sold me my new car. We got talking and I related a story about Nova Scotia. He immediately asked where and I told him. He said wait a second and he phones his aged mother and asked her if she knew the family name. Now get this she worked in partnership with the member of the family. Put that one together, What are the chances of pulling that close a connection together out of the blue? Destiny pure destiny. This person was sent to touch my life, a message will pass and no doubt we will move on.

I will give yet another example; I had a chance meeting with a friend I used to go to school with. Her late husband was declined a membership in an organization that he previously had a membership. There was no apparent reason for this decline, other than one of the key players didn't like him. After hearing this, I believed an apology was in order, it will mean nothing to her late husband but it will set the record straight that he was worthy. Corrective action has been taken.

My mother's parents had a blonde stereo. My grandfather would hear us walking by that machine and he was on our case not to touch it. No matter what we did in that room we were not allowed near that stereo. This all changed when my aunt burnt the top of it with a cigarette. Karma works in mysterious ways. Was there ever a true forgiveness from my grandfather probably not.

When I was in my early twenties I was walking down a street. I slipped and fell and nipped the end of my one finger off on the ice. To this day I couldn't tell you anything different, I got up and brushed myself off, then noticing the blood all over the place. Was it just a freak accident? But if you couple it with other freak accidents was it. My dad's father lost the same fingertip to a freak accident. Two of my dad's brothers lost a fingertip to freak accidents. Now you have a trend. Were we all clumsy? I would like to think not.

The end result will be felt. It is not to penalize someone rather to restore faith. There will be only a handful of people, key people that will experience this seed planted but the ramifications are endless.

> *"You suppose you are the trouble, But you are the cure. You suppose that you are the lock on the door but you are the key that opens it. It's too bad that you want to be someone else. You don't see your own face, your own beauty. Yet, no face is more beautiful than yours" --- Rumi*

> *"The teacher who is indeed wise does not bid you to enter the house of his wisdom but rather leads you to the threshold of your mind." - Kahlil Gibran*

CHAPTER FOUR

# The End

I have had people ask "What is it like to see a person die". All I can say, at any given time it has to be respected as a private thing. We come into this world alone and leave it the same way. Contrary to popular belief most people don't get to see a natural death first hand. My first wife's sister came to help in her final months; she was at her side every possible minute and vowed to be there for her passing. The day she started down her final mile, her other sister came to pay her respects. I told her to spend as much time with her as she needed. This she did, then the two sisters decided to take a break and my mother, my son's wife at that time and myself went into the room. I talked to her and said I could go no further the rest was up to her and she was gone. The first reaction was "Why were we to be the ones there at that particular time?" I believe she couldn't do it with any other combination of people in the room.

When my father passed, the family was with him, providing the support off and on for nearly seven months. I was by his side almost continuous for the last month and a half. He was removed to Palliative Care because family burn-out was showing its signs. He still had the round the clock vigil in the hospital but on his last evening we decided to have a family dinner with everyone together. He choose that time to pass, when he was alone.

Dad struggle through the last months of his life were filled with dramatic emotional events that will stay with any participants as long as they live. The nurses from Palliative Care were so astounded by the teamwork and family dedication that they asked if we could write a book on our experience to assist others dealing with the same problems. To date that hasn't happened, we can talk about it but the words haven't hit paper yet. Dad's cancer was in his large intestine, he went through extreme discomfort prior to acknowledging he had a problem. By the time, the doctors decided he had the problem he was already past the point of no return. He was placed in the hospital, and we were advised to get his affairs in order, which we did. A couple days later, he left the hospital and vowed he had other things in mind. He came home to live out his last days to his dignified standard. We setup a special room for him, set out to make his last days the best. We were well into the fall and winter was fast approaching. One day we noticed a Ladybug walking across his headboard, wrong season, it was removed. The next day same thing, this happened every day until he was moved to the hospital in late January. Every time any of the family sees a ladybug to this day they remark "Grandpa came for a visit". There are several other stories that relate to the ladybug after dad's passing, all remarkable as the first.

This by no means the first time an animal or bird or pet has come into the presence of a dying person to help move through the grief. My first wife as she was going through her final phase had a bond with our old dog that in the end the dog had to be put down because it lost all bodily functions. His ashes were spread over the foot of her gravesite.

My mother's mom loved hummingbirds; she related they had a special meaning in her life. Just by the nature of the person she was, she was one that would not come right out and say that her experiences with hummingbirds had a spiritual influence on her life. But we all knew the feelings felt.

I have related this story many times to different people and inevitably someone will have one of their own experiences to relate back.

My cousin, taken from us at an early age, suffered his own agony with bone cancer after a simple fall from a bike. He was commonly called an affectionate tease, who loved knowing people. One beautiful trait was helping everyone, wherever possible. While in the hospital and working through is agonizing life he was told to scream, yell or just vent his anger. His calm remark was "I have nothing to complain about". His life influenced mine over the seed he planted in his dignity and courage.

We all have our destinies; we all have our mile to walk. What we do and how we achieve it, is ours and only ours. Outside influences are only that, the choices we make put us on the path long or short to the ultimate end. Some paths take us through hardships, others joy. We all hit rock bottom at least six times in our life, each time is supposed to open our hearts and take us closer to God. We have to learn to love ourselves and build his temple within ourselves. Then and only then can you experience true love.

Our family knows divorce as well as any other. We know the ramifications and scars left behind. My father always said "Get out of one bed, before you get in another!!" He was not a man with many theories on life but that one to me is one of his best. I have followed that theory all my life. Another seed planted.

I marvel at how some people manage to apply the right names to the right people after their endless relationships. One of my mother's quotes is "If you don't have a variety of experiences young, you do it when you're older!" It is not meant to give you permission to do absolutely anything your little ole heart desires rather date several people young to ensure you end up with the type of person you want.

Unity is the realization that at the deepest level everyone shares the same consciousness; these are the seeds of all love and joy. We all carry the trait to be right. If you let this trait dominate your relationship, you are turning your back on love and your ultimate lasting unity. An open heart allows the power of communication in, for two entities to come to a common ground and to understand the other person's point of view. There are times when a compromise is far more beneficial than an outright legislated "I am right". Many times we look to deep for a problem that doesn't exist, taking time to actually hear what has been said not what you think you heard is crucial. We make the bed we lie in and if it is filled with negative feelings, nothing good is going to come from it and this can carry on from here to eternity till the attitude changes. Another Seed, One in which everyone should plant.

The top question in any healthy discussion is "What gives me the right to Judge?" If you can honestly answer that question, your mind will take you to a similar situation where you too could have been judged. I know now as I move deeper into the last phase of life, the spiritual phase, this book has to be written. If my knowledge helps one person, I have accomplished what I set out to achieve. My life of helping people will be complete. Another seed planted.

Ironically, once read and if you are moved, even just a little bit the heart will take the next step. Your future steps, will not be in fear, rather knowing we are placed on earth to experience some pain, this is what makes us humble. To error is human, it is what we do to correct our actions afterwards that count. If we ignore or compound the mistake our hearts only harden and the joy soon leaves for a life of aches, pains and illness.

I thought our 1992 dilemma with so many people dying in the same year was a test. I recently shared this story with a friend who had a similar experience in their family. Their numbers were greater, their experiences similar for the mind blown feelings felt. Which leads to the statement walk a mile in my shoes and we shall relate. At that moment I did and we did relate. One is bad enough at any given time but several the mind just doesn't want to process this information. Some small families absolutely will never have to walk this path.

I remember my estranged wife told me away back that she went and talked to my first wife's headstone. I thought it was quite sincere at the time but apparently it must have only been "lip service". To me if you are talking to someone that has passed on you are indirectly talking to the maker himself. It was his master plan that brought the person home in the first place however it may have happened. Their purpose here on earth was complete.

I just watched the movie "My Sister's Keeper" by myself and if that wasn't a flashback into desperate times. I felt the roller coaster of emotions, they experienced and the pain endured by the family. I related through my own experiences, where driving down the road after a bout of chemo my first wife was barfing out the window, struggling to maintain her dignity before she made it home. The extreme summer heat and chemo were not a nice combination at the best of times it ripped the heart out to witness the suffering experienced just to extend life that short period of time.

Have you ever noticed that so many deaths happen in threes, I seen this do many times it is hard to understand the reasoning behind it. This is something worth watching,

*Eyes Closed, Too Hear*

I see two that are sitting on the threshold in my family and the prognosis is sooner than later but it is there. To think that there could be another to round off the three is beyond all thought but will it stand true yet again is another thing. That is another unfortunate factor that seems to standout more in larger families. Everything seems to cyclical. The only thing with death age is not a factor that cares the major weight in the outcome. Same as sickness it is not partial who it strikes at any given time.

My mother has a statement that she uses more than not and it really rips my you know what. It is "Next year when I am gone", it doesn't matter where or when it comes out. It urks me, I know my sisters' all feel the same. We all use statements that turn other people's heads, but one must think "Is that how I want to be remembered after I am gone?" It is not like this is going to be a real surprise for her to see it in print; we have had several conversations about this particular statement. Is this a seed we want to plant for further generations? I think not. My youngest son has the right attitude he wants to live to be a hundred. He has said that over and over again since he was a little boy. To me, I would be happy with eighty five, I think I have the health to get me that far. We can see these types of faults in other people's makeup, yet fail drastically at recognizing it within ourselves. But one has to think where these types of statements come from other than a learned behaviour from life itself. My sister coins the phrase "What makes mama happy, makes us all happy" with a look of intrepid frustration written on her face. As I will say many times throughout this book, we have to learn to love ourselves before we can openly have these feelings change in others.

My youngest sister has said to me she will cease to live after my mother is gone. This again is a statement, that if you allow it to live in your sub conscious mind will only manifest and move slowly into the lives of everyone around us. Death is like birth it is a phase of life, we must grasp and recognize as our next step. We don't need to force the issue; it is already in our destiny. Fulfill your purpose here on earth; be remembered in dignity and then you one's purpose can plant the true seed meant to be left behind.

I have always been partial to oak trees, you often don't see many in the west but if I had a opportunity to plant a tree by my headstone. It would be an oak tree. When I first joined the military, it was mandatory that we attended church services every Sunday. Starting off in the Navy, the "Heart of Oak" was played every service; it was another hymn that did a number on me. I was moved by the music as much as the words.

On my recent trip to Massachusetts I marvelled at the number of oak trees that I seen there. This thought played with me after my return. I knew I was to be back there again and thought I would investigate this further. My youngest son and I had an opportunity to combine research and the family tree into our trip of the Maritimes and to our surprise we found several long lost relatives buried under oak trees. There under the mighty oak we found the headstones of Great grandparents and GG grandparents on my mother's side in two separate cemeteries for sure. If there is something that was part of another life that came to me in a seed an oak tree had to be part of it that's for sure. It was fantastic to have another generation with me, in this discovery. The first hand observance passed to my son will no doubt follow him well into his later years where he may share the experience with another. There has to be more to the mighty oak and its perfect shaped seeds. Will I ever truly find out more than I now know or is it meant for another to solve? Time will tell.

*Eyes Closed, Too Hear*

I feel I got to pick up a lost piece to the puzzle and moved it back into play. I had the opportunity to spend quality time with my son, sharing the moments that may have helped form his heritage. Is he the one that needs to take this to its next step? There is a reason why we had to do this together. Thus another seed is planted.

RJ Woodward

## Heart of Oak

*Come cheer up, my lads! 'tis to glory we steer,*
*To add something more to this wonderful year;*
*To honour we call you, not press you like slaves,*
*For who are so free as the sons of the waves?*

*Chorus*

*Heart of oak are our ships, heart of oak are our men;*
*We always are ready, steady, boys, steady!*
*We'll fight and we'll conquer again and again.*

*We ne'er see our foes but we wish them to stay,*
*They never see us but they wish us away;*
*If they run, why we follow, and run them ashore,*
*For if they won't fight us, we cannot do more.*

*Chorus*

*They swear they'll invade us, these terrible foes,*
*They frighten our women, our children, and beaus;*
*But should their flat bottoms in darkness get o'er,*
*Still Britons they'll find to receive them on shore.*

*Chorus*

*We'll still make them fear, and we'll still make them flee,*
*And drub 'em on shore, as we've drubb'd 'em at sea;*
*Then cheer up, my lads! with one heart let us sing:*
*Our soldiers, our sailors, our statesmen and Queen.*

*Chorus*

*Eyes Closed, Too Hear*

*The music to Heart of Oak was by Dr. William Boyce (1711-1779). The English words were written by the famous actor David Garrick (1716-1779) in 1759.*

> *"We die to each other daily. What we know of other people is only our memory of the moments during which we knew them. And they have changed since then" --- T.S. Eliot*

## Chapter Five

# Romance

Too many people enter marriage for all the wrong reasons. The first thing any person has to realize there will be a day when the "LUST" is gone. Believe it, Accept It. Pray that you have grown to accept and meet the vows you made to bind your marriage. Today's Trade-In society has gotten so complex that many of these values are readily exchanged for short term satisfaction. It is far too easy to blame everyone, but the right person. If you don't deal with these deficiencies now, you deal with them later. You can only move them from relationship to relationship so long before they come back to haunt. The heart has to be open, to like yourselves. If you don't like yourself, a strong relationship will never exist. period. To me, emotional confusion is worse than death. Death is final, and everyone heals. Emotional confusion is like an endless roller-coaster you can't get off until corrective action is taken. Many people in this state don't realize this until they have hurt countless people in the process.

 I have said it once and I will say it again a marriage is bringing two different people from two different walks of life to blend and form their own version of companionship that carries on into the next generations. There are struggles. These challenges are what make the bond work. If there are no values, the children take the same traits into their relationships. Thus the downward spiral until the cycle is broken. It takes a strong dedicated couple with ethical values to break the cycle and change their path and purpose in life.

    I am a survivor of a marriage that went astray after sixteen years. A marriage that stopped the same day and time as my first marriage, for reasons I can't even comprehend. I know the steps I have taken to ensure that if there were faults in my traits I will correct before I take them into another relationship. My wedding vows meant everything to me, too link them to the final date of my first marriage is beyond anything that I can ever imagine. There is a meaning, there is a purpose and I know it has taken me into Spiritual realization that will take me through the rest of my life. The pains we suffer here on earth, will prepare us for the next phase of our life. I can only ensure my heart is open to prepare for it. I never thought after sixteen years, seventeen now, that I would be dealing with the "D" word. I heard from day one how men only thought with their "weenies" and lusted for anything that had two bumps on their chest. Maybe not realizing that wasn't that important to me where my first wife had everything removed in a valiant attempt to conquer her cancer. A person who was so vain, she wouldn't leave the house without her lipstick so perfectly in place. A person whose chest was so scarred from radiation the pain really never ceased. It is one thing to be a hypocrite, but another to not realize that you are doing it. After all is said and done I will only accept the truth as grounds for this demise, irreconcilable differences is not an option in my mind. A mutated seed planted by satin's hand to further corrupt the Garden of Eden.

    Having spent many hour alone, working through my levels of grief I have learned I am not truly alone. Doors open slowly to let the Sun back in, my ultimate purpose to face my demons and to embrace my shortcomings, has given me the opportunity to enhance my life. Now back in control of my own destiny, my heart open to receive its ultimate joy. I will walk my road and continue to touch the people near and dear to me.

I know I have unfinished business. I have placed my life in the hands of my maker and with the preparations required to further my life slowly starting to take shape. The road ahead is no longer dark. What a great feeling, I openly accept each day, the forgiveness I prayed for has come in ways beyond belief. The forgiveness not given can remain with the people to burden to realize, but I am OK with it. The monkey is off my back and I walk at with a happier stride. There is not enough money in the world to buy this feeling. It comes from the heart. From an open heart far beyond any riches and monetary value.

Too strive for unconditional love is still a goal in my life. The learning process has been long and hard. My faith in people makes me believe it is truly attainable. This will be either in this lifetime or the next, the lessons learned will bear fruit and I will have the companionship I desire until eternity. With that kind of faith in mankind, an open heart and the seed plant, I proceed along my path.

I can honestly say, I have lived through an existence where I felt my life was being erased before my eyes. Anything that symbolized me was disappearing. Then I realized this was only one person's doing, my life cannot be erased. That was when I realized I had given away the control of my life to please another person. I had given away a chunk of my soul to another person. It was there I realized we have to Love ourselves before we can let love into our heart. Once I grasped that and believed it, did my heart feel like mine again? I realized the numerous areas I had touched in my life, the many people I had extended friendship and a helping hand to. I realized my life wasn't finished and I had many other people I had to share my "Seeds of Life "with. These are the seeds that move through generations. The seeds will come back for years to come, to move someone else to their warm and fuzzy spot. I proceed knowing I wasn't a loser after all, for what I gain no person can erase.

I mentioned we emotionally hit rock bottom at least six times in our lives. I can honestly relate to four times, each time there was something revitalizing happened. One with the most significant impact on me was when my first wife was dying. We had gone through endless drilling, mind draining questions and countless hallucinations mainly due to the strong drugs used to dull the pain. I had reached the end of my tether and needed a break. I went outside the hospital and looked up the wind was blowing hard, the branches were bowing down to the ground, the skies were wild. All I could do has howler out "Make It Stop.. OH Lord.... Make It Stop". Everything went quiet, the trees stopped swaying, I went back to her room and there was never another foul outburst again from her lips. And she survived for several weeks after that. An antidote to this my wife was placed in the same room my grandfather had died in several years earlier. His memories were so engrained in my mind I had to have her moved to a different room. So believe me when I say "Words expressed harshly, do leave a mark" they do come back when we least expect it. If we don't deal with it in the here and now, it will creep back in to bite our butt at our weakest moment.

There is one thing that I heard so many times in my second marriage, a statement that I could never totally grasp and to this day it remains one that bites deep. It is "Your Job" to me a marriage, a relationship, a whatever is not a job, sorry to me a relationship is two individuals working together for the common good. Period, you are meant to offset each other in everything you do. If the input is not equal, then the output can be far less than the same. I always felt I have pulled my weight and then some. I have been available, my standards are mine and I take pride in the ability to satisfy almost any request. I have been able to care for myself all my life, but the feeling of being viewed below someone else's standards just doesn't play right with me.

    To be raised with the idea that you are better than most is really a sin in its own right. Everything that someone else has always must play havoc on one's mind, when you feel you are above them the comparisons and competition remains above all foremost in your mind. How can you ever treat anyone as your equal when you run in such delusions? To this end many live beyond their means trying to keep up or be better. What are we doing for our future generations? A seed I really don't want to see planted or should I dare say a weed that is allowed to run rampant with no value for other life.

> *"Let others lead small lives, but not you. Let others argue over small things, but not you. Let others cry over small hurts, but not you. Let others leave their future in someone else's hands, but not you."* ~ Jim Rohn

CHAPTER SIX

# Heritage

From dad's family there is only two sisters left. One Aunt a leap year baby, can turn your head with a story to this day. She can have you in stitches, with tears running down your cheeks in a heartbeat. I regret that I haven't taken the time to write some of these stories down because once she's gone another page of history will be gone. We often say we should do this, but procrastinating for tomorrow seems to always win. We have no guarantee, what tomorrow will bring. If I had to do everything over, I probably wouldn't change that much, but I would pay closer attention to the finer details of life.

Mom has a younger brother left, he is another that followed in his father's footprints and worked with the CNR until he retired. We have that quality that if our paths don't cross for several years we can pick up where we left off and continue on.

I have four sons, three carry my last name and one step-son. My two oldest sons have long gone their own ways. The oldest was born hearing-handicapped, due to his mother being exposed to rubella during her pregnancy. His life has taken him from a childhood marriage with two children to a life deeper engrained in the world of the deaf. I have no problem with that. I only wish we had better communication skills.

My second oldest son has two children and has followed in my footsteps with a career in the military. He like his father has done a world of travel throughout his career. For a person that had a problem with my life he sure is walking the same mile very closely. Again, I relate back to one of my first points, the seeds we plant throughout our lives keep reappearing in later generations.

These two boys in their early years could turn any situation into trouble. I remember taking them along with my mother's parents to the Bay to by some wool. My grandmother loved to knit. Anyway we are looking through these various bins of wool to turn around to see these two taking the wrappers off a whole bin of wool. Of course corrective action needed to happen, one step towards them and they were gone knocking over a couple racks of clothes in the process. This was the norm, for a couple years. If that seed was planted to bear fruit, there should be a few good stories that can supplement this paragraph.

My step-son entered my life shortly after his third birthday. We aspired to play tricks on him in his earlier years. It was nothing to slip on and scare him with a Halloween mask. This one time we decided to celebrate our Halloween at this historical fort in BC, needless to say it was blacker than black and hands and bodies jumped out at every turn. Putting it simple I don't know how he ever slept a night after that event. His school years were not his forte, he is an outside person and now in the working world, strives to do exactly that. He has a potential, if anchored will give him a very rewarding life. To me there is a purpose why he entered my life for this period of time. I would like to think it was to give him an anchor in life. Maybe his well needed sense of stability. The couple times he got in trouble I was the one sitting at the table with him. I was his spokesman, his anchor, his direction to the end result.

*Eyes Closed, Too Hear*

My youngest son was the child that I really had ample time to spend with. Merely due to the fact I was retired and had the time to dedicate to his younger years. I believe he has experienced more in life at his age than many other children. I admire his gentle nature and his ability to get along with almost anyone. I foresee a future for him that will no doubt be extremely rewarding in its own right. To stifle his inner drive would be a sin, his potentials are only starting to blossom. He said to me the other day, they make movies out of anything these days. Wouldn't it be funny if they made one from your book? Pausing he added but they would probably have to kill you off in the end.

He along with a school friend developed a new hand gesture known as "The Clank" during the time when H1N1 was at its peak. It was very ingenious to say the least and at the yearend festivities it was remarked on as one of the accomplishments noted during that school year. If this type of potential can be seen at this age who knows what is in store for the future.

During a recent discussion with his mother, I related how fast things will change for him in the next few years; you can see it now as he strives for his independence. I related how I could easily move on and finish what I am destined to do with what is left in my life. There was a level of shock that set her back but the truth is there also. When you sit idly by waiting to be called on to serve a function and that call really never comes is there any other reason to sit and wait. I can do things I need to do with what is left in my life and find dedicated time when we can be together also.

I can see a level of good in everyone, but if someone isn't putting on a true front I can see through that also. I have guided my family away from people that I question until they win my trust. I have asked strange kids to leave because they are rifling through the kitchen drawers. Small things on the surface but if there has to be a lesson learned, that is the easiest way to get it across. Confront it head on; otherwise it just eats away at you.

## Chapter Seven

# Hidden Facts

You look back on dad's side his grandparents both died of consumption. As you look at the different family trees and sometimes you can find the cause of death in the documentation. We live in a great time because modern technology allows us access to almost anything, information is at our fingertips. Dad came from a line of bakers, I have a sister that is a Celiac and since she has been diagnosed there has been several others. Nobody in days gone by would have thought a family of bakers would have a flour related problem, but we can today. Knees and joints are also a problem on my father's side. Heart, cholesterol and eyes are on my mother's.

The information is usually staring us in the face and we are too blind to see. Our lives are too hectic to follow the finer things in life. We need to stop. Walk with an open heart, feel the power of the spirit we all hold the seeds to. If we could do that and embrace our humble destiny the world would be a better place.

There are things that I feel have been guiding me all my life. I am looking for a direction that has plagued me, I just never had the resources to see the vision I was meant to follow. I know whatever I was meant to do is close at hand. The things I know are so definite, the things I feel are so unique. I now know whatever happens from this day forward I will be guided with the faith planted within me. I feel so humbled to be afforded the insight to hear my aspirations recognized. To see a prayer answered sixty years in the making a prayer, that is giving me a whole new direction.

There are times I feel I gave away my power by placing others ahead of me. Now know a person can be only your equal in life to walk beside you not ahead or behind. To raise them in praise is one thing but to put them on a pedestal where they feel they are higher than you can only lead to trouble. It is there we lose our control and purpose in life. So many times I have seen where people have allowed themselves to be pushed to a point where they lose their self respect. The inner glow merely disappears.

I have known right from a little boy the hymns I would like played at my funeral. To be that predestined is beyond belief. There is a reason; I am certain a reason that has been placed there long ago. These hymns were made up from part of my own selection for other family members. I don't mind sharing they just express me. "Then Sings My Soul", "In the Garden" and "Amazing Grace" if these are played after I am gone, I would believe my life was a success. It will be a time for celebration to a rich and fulfilled life not in monies rather life experiences.

It is not that I am ridged or set in my ways; I am truly very easy to get along with sometimes too easy, where observers remark I allow people to get away with too much. I only treat people how I like to be treated until they hurt me. Then it becomes my option where it goes from there. Hurt me once, I'm the fool and I will repent. Hurt me twice, you are the fool and I will forgive. Do it again I walk away and it remains your problem not mine. You get to deal with it and find your own solutions. Remain blind to the fact; the heart will never open to feel the glory that it can hold.

Coincidences, my middle sister related one to be that I feel worthy of sharing. I have stated there are dates that repeat throughout history. My sister graduated from her career training May 29, her daughter graduated many years later from college May 29 and finally her son graduated this year on May 29. This situation isn't the first one I have seen numerous example in working through our family tree.

No matter what it is, if one person is running with the information and the other don't have access to it. We are dealing with hidden facts, facts that makes one feel more superior or righteous. Unfortunately this fact is only in the mind of the one holding the cards, it does and it will come back to haunt. The truth has a way of balancing everything out.

We never get to know all the facts at the same time, each one of us express ourselves in different ways. We disseminate information in different ways, we give the highlights and once questions are asked we then start to fill in the gaps. There is nothing wrong with this, it is natural. There are hidden facts with everything; it also indicates a level of trust. How often do we walk up to a stranger on the street and start to relate our life story? On the same token, if we went to see a councillor do we spill the beans on the first seating? No, it takes months of visitations before we allow people into our inner circle our top most secrets. It takes a very rare person to walk right in and be able to get to that in depth point of our heart where the real facts lie. The hidden facts that help make up the fibre of our inner being.

My mother has this unique quality, she can drive by a person's house and get the feeling she should drop in and see how things are. Nine chances out of ten that person will say I was just thinking about you, have you got time to stop for a minute. And before she has left, a hidden fact is shared that makes a difference in that person's day. This is Great!! Fantastic to be able to achieved that level of trust in the people around you.

The seed that is shared is one that is so rare; many will never get to see the fruit of this marvel in their lifetime. Truly unfortunate, so one should appreciate this quality if you have experienced this feeling. For you are truly blessed.

Another hidden fact, I like to call the "Seven Year Itch" at one time it was only referred to something a man felt after seven years of being with the same woman. In today's weird society it is something that happens to both sexes. We have made it sociably acceptable to show infatuation to another at any given time, not realizing the ramifications or the people we hurt in the process. To coin another phrase "Fish or cut bait" either you realize the same problems will exist in another relationship or you just walk away and gamble the next time is going to be better. The action taken has consequences if clouded with a tarnished heart. The same wandering eye will be back in another seven years. This is a seed I can plant and will stand behind to watch it bear its sour fruit. Sour fruit because more than one always gets hurt and it isn't the one with the itch.

During my recent trip I had the opportunity to talk to a gentleman while sitting in the hot tub. I related to writing a book and of course he wanted to know more detail. I expressed the highlights behind my book and this lead to a whole series of conversation that would never have taken place otherwise. Each story expressed was interpreted also with his own story; I realized that was exactly what I was trying to achieve in my writing. Here was a hidden fact with total realization on my part. He asked me if I had ever heard quotes that he thought were synonymous to only his life and many I could relate to. Why again were we to meet? To have a chance meeting, if only to reaffirm what I was trying to express in my book. To know it can be offered to the public without the thought of any value to someone else.

The message I want to pass, the seed as per say; the introduction to a person that is trying to piece their life into having a genuine purpose. This can only be measured by the reaction of others. I feel I have gained the knowledge to keep moving ahead.

We all have stubborn traits to some extent but I have a couple nephews that have pushed it to the limit. Tying shoes is a good example to use; they said they would not learn to tie shoes until they started school and they didn't. One walked out of his bedroom on his first day of school with his shoes tied. He knew how to do it the whole time but felt no requirement to share his newly acquired talent.

> *"You can tell whether a man is clever by his answers... You can tell whether a man is wise by his questions."* Naguib Mahfouz

## Chapter Eight

# To Judge

One of my biggest flaws has been "Being to Judgemental", it is now my ambition to remove this flaw from my character. It is a part of my daily prayers to ask that this fault be removed from my life and like any constant repeat ion I find I take corrective action if it slips out. I will master this fault. I have always been the type of person that says it as they see it. That action walks hand in hand with being judgemental.

Dad's second oldest brother sat my mother down after they were married and related to her that one of the worst traits of this family was the level of trust or jealousy. It was one of the worst flaws and its stigma goes back several generations. I believe the seed was planted away back when my grandfather was conceived out of wedlock. This past secret has been so well buried that only the ones practising genealogy have been able to unearth a couple sparse references.

When I say my daily prayers I asked that this flaw be removed from the family and not affect any further generations. That's a seed I really want planted. It is amazing how far out of sync the sub-conscious mind is to the conscious mind. As we plant our seeds and through constant repetition the two spheres come into sync and our ability transform these wants to become a habit. Once they are a habit, the change becomes so transparent to the open heart it becomes a natural way of life. The key factor to all this, is a mind has to stay positive. When you choose to dwell in the negative, all the desire in the world will not change you. This is a very simple fact that takes work and persistence to achieve. Know It. Believe It.

We often find ourselves in situations where we perceive to see something that isn't there. If we play it over and over in our minds till it becomes a problem we then have become judgemental. Every action taken thereafter can only open further animosity which festers to jealousy. It is at that point, we must stop and find corrective action because from there it will continue to go bad. Any words expressed, are words that are out there to rattle and slice clear to the heart. Where words expressed cannot return from where they came. Where in as much as we would like to see this happen. This only leads to further words, expressed over other actions that kill the spirit of the recipient. Harsh words expressed in haste are just as sharp as any double edged sword once it cuts the heart. The scars remain.

We can love our children and take a lot of bitter words from what they say in haste. But if a spouse does the same, their demise is clear at hand if they don't realize their mistakes and correct this behaviour right away. There is a point where enough is enough. They are not blood and allegiances don't run that deep. I have seen brother and sister make the same mistake over harsh words and be estranged for a period of time. Some family relationships may never be the same. Make sure this action is not yours, before you think to judge for what you lose you may not get back. Only transfer it to your next relationship. Open your heart and destroy that trait forever. You will be a better person for it.

My first wife's sister didn't talk to her father for ten years. That was ten years lost as far as I can see. When all was said and done they couldn't remember what the problem was that caused the rift in the first place. I have seen this type of action on more than one occasion, my dad's sister and her husband left on ugly terms after my grandmother's death. But they resolved their differences with my dad later in life and maybe were stronger for it in the end. Who knows? But it was still time lost till they found themselves again.

    This vice is so easy to fall into; to pass an opinion on a person is really a judgement on that person. We are all guilty of this, no matter how we look at it. This is what makes us like or dislike a person. This is what attracts us or makes us repel a person after mere minutes together. We judge, it is a built in defence mechanism to protect our private space. Once we destroy this, it is extremely hard to restore, that is human nature. It takes a very special person to take a person back into their trust after they have wronged you.

    Time can correct almost anything. Like with the statement so often heard if you love a person set them free, if it was meant to be they will come back. The key is if this happens don't allow negative judgement to rule the final decision. View your decision from an open heart; let this feeling manifest the love that was meant to be. This love is the power of our maker at work, placing the destiny he has outlined for us to follow. Make the path clouded with judgement and one gets to follow a long struggling road to the final outcome rather than the path outlined for one pure of heart.

    Another leaf has fallen from our tree, not from a death but from a weaker footing to the basic foundation. A marriage that the dust hadn't settled on the gifts received not quite a year ago. I firmly believe when two become one they have to work together in a union of trust and understanding. Our modern conveniences offer quick access to a myriad of avenues to communicate to everyone rather than the ones closest to us. These modern communications can also be the worst vices in a relationship, no feeling, no heart or no conscious. One cannot judge in this situation, there were vices on both sides. To point fingers in either direction would be easy, to judge a temptation. Bottom-line a marriage that started on unstable grounds and the foundation caved in on them because the ability to work together wasn't established.

Our family is very unique, over the years we have evolved into the League of Nations. My mother's father had great difficulty with the thought of mixing cultures into the family. The changes we have seen have all transpired since his passing. I can't even bring my mind to think where we would be if his beliefs were to be passed down to the future generations. One seed, I am glad to see was not planted.

> *Who are you to judge the life I live? I am not perfect and I don't live to be, but before you start pointing fingers, make sure your hands are clean. ~ BOB MARLEY*

> *"People who judge are caught in fear, and do not know who they are..." --- R.G. Wolf*

## Chapter Nine

# Pets

Dogs, we have always had a family dog. Each member of the family has had a dog, a companion, a pet to curl up at their feet and hopefully sleep. Now with every pet, there is a story, they go right back to my dad's father and his Irish Setters. These animals could never do no wrong, Hah! My grandfather fell asleep on his settee in the living room. There was a large roast on the dining room table ready to be placed in the oven for the evening meal. Needless to say when he woke up all that was left was a small scrap of brown paper and a very contented dog. There was on quick trip to the locker plant to get another so my grandmother wouldn't know. Another story, same dog, grandfather had to give very important presentation at Masons. He laid out his Masonic garb, prim and proper on the bed. He polished his shoes to a high shine and left to do something else; when he returned the toes were missing off both shoes. This time he had to get the owner of the local shoe store to open the store to replace his shoes prior to his meeting.

    I remember as a child I would ride the one Irish setter as my horse. One day I ran away from home, took the Irish setter and was found sometime later asleep on the dog's back just wondering up and down the streets.

    We had an Irish setter for a short period of time, until it ran down the basement steps and knocked the trapdoor

*Eyes Closed, Too Hear*

down on my sister's hand breaking several fingers. It was decided to be too high spirited for town life and was sent to the farm. After that we went through a series of smaller dogs, starting with a black cocker spaniel. My dad and that dog never seen eye to eye.

In Nova Scotia, I had a basset hound who with one swipe of his tail could clear the coffee table and not bat an eye. He became so possessive of his territory that he had to move on for the safety of the neighbourhood kids. Our next dog was in Winnipeg, he was a French poodle cross. He was my first wife's dog, we never hit it off. He had epileptic fits and I would hold him down so he wouldn't hurt himself. I got nipped so many times I don't dare to guess how many. I remember we took him when we went to visit my oldest sister and her family one time. We went out for a short period of time and this dog literally destroyed the front porch area, floor, door, everything. He did survive till first wife died.

We had another poodle cross, a much smaller dog, she came with us from BC to Alberta. One day a cat ran through the yard and she was in hot pursuit. All we hear was a screech of tires and a whoomp. We ran out to see her immobile on the road, I picked her up thinking she would literally tear my arm off, but the look of compassion in her eyes absolutely melted my heart. She never made a sound, we had her rebuilt and she was with us for a couple more years till a brain aneurysm synched her fate. The look of such complete trust as she was taken away was so moving, I to this day still have difficulty thinking about it.

I was talking to a member of the family and asked if they had any other dog stories they would like to share. I gather my dad had bought a new pair of work boots and he set them by the door for the next day's work. My parents went out to visit friends and when they got home they found a pair of spats because the top was chewed right off the boots. To take this one step further my nephew got a new pair of Oakley sunglasses and the same deal his little pup had rearranged the design considerably.

Yes we have pets, each in their own right a personality onto their own, they demand attention. They try to talk, they watch TV, and you would sometimes wonder who's in charge. I always say my next dog is going to be ceramic and low and behold in comes another personality to raise and walk as a proud member of the family.

Birds, we had budgies as we were growing up, they would fly around the Living room and sit on top of the blinds. Blue Boy and Pretty Boy, one blue of course the other green. One evening, dad brought home a couple friends; they were all a wee bit under the weather. A few more drinks were taken and one of the budgies got brave enough to land on the rim of one of the friend's glass. They all laughed, we kids thought it was great. The budgie pooped in the glass as it was shooed away and before we could get a word in edgewise the drink was gone. None be known to the recipient. It has remained a good laugh all these years later.

My young niece has always shown an interest in animals, so she followed this interest into her career has a veterinary assistant. When she was young and living on their family farm, she was readily called on to help with the cattle. On this one occasion she delivered this calf that became her shadow. It followed her everywhere, slept on the deck with the dog and played Frisbee like the dog, until he ate her mother's flowers and was banished to the corrals with the rest of the cattle.

On returning from my recent trip, I took my son back to his mother's place. The three dogs greeted me like I was their long lost salvation and I realized how they must feel. They never asked to be removed from their prior living arrangement but yet they have no ability to express their wants either. I found this hurt, brought back several suppressed feelings and I had to leave. Why could an animal with so called limited intelligence, express so much care and compassion for a human that in their eyes has deserted them? The throw-away dad, that left them behind. They carry a level of trust and compassion far greater than the humans caring for them. What are we missing in our lives and we don't see? It is these types of compassion I am more attuned to as of late. My In-laws recently lost their family pet of many years. They are having a great problem adjusting to life without it and when questioned if they would ever get another their response was simple. "No, we don't want the pet to outlive us!!" different approach, but theirs. Living alone, I know the void in my life not having one around.

> *"A human being is a part of the whole called by us 'universe', a part limited in time and space. He experiences himself, his thoughts and feelings as something separated from the rest ... a kind of optical illusion of his consciousness. Our task must be to free ourselves from this prison by widening our circle of compassion to embrace all living creatures and all nature in its beauty"* ~ *Albert Einstein*

## Chapter Ten

# Military

It is amazing to see how the military as placed its mark on a family. My dad's father was in WWI. My dad, his older brother and several uncles served in WWII. My cousin and I served in the regular force for a full career and my second oldest son and his wife are serving now.

Military was in my blood from an early age, I did four years of Air Cadets along with my cousin prior to enlisting in the regular forces. We travelled more with the Air Cadets than many of our friends did through half their lifetimes. We got to see the Seattle World Fair; thinking at the time there was nothing better. We were young and adventuresome. My cousin is a couple years older than me but I joined the regular force a year before he did. He finished his education and I didn't.

My siblings all remarked about how I used to rearrange the fridge or deep freeze to chill my boots to put the perfect high gloss shine on for the next parade. At least times have changed and there is a higher quality of polish available now. Mind you I don't polish my shoes to that degree anymore either.

I have had some of the greatest experiences in my life while serving in the military. It is said that everyone has a double in this world. I had the opportunity to meet one such individual that was taken for me all the time. I could never see any real resemblances but so many mixed us up all the time. They would swear we were doubles. Amazing what is seen by the human eye, yet not seen.

To change anything NO, here we are a good many years later, the Canadian Navy is celebrating its 100$^{th}$ and I am viewed as one of the oldest Navy members in our Legion. My how time flies. I have been asked to help celebrate this event by carrying the white ensign on the Legion float later on this summer. To fit in with the occasion, I have taken the liberty to grow a beard.

It is really amazing how much the military touches our day to day life. We see examples of personal sacrifice, how one person has offered their life so others can remain free. So our lifestyle as we know it remains intact. We support our troops with flags and ribbons, locally and afar. We each show our support in our own way and encourage our young to remember the sacrifices offered so they may remain free. To know how long this will last is up to our society and future generations. What mistakes could upset this fine balance of peace in this mixed up world. Yes, the military is very much a part of our day to day lives. Know it and believe it.

The Legion is the epitome of comradeship. It is one organization that recognizes a person who offered up their life for their country. Here is an organization that recognizes men of such courage where they volunteer to die thousands of miles from home, who scramble to save each other when the bullets were flying, and they can still smile about it. To ensure future generations could live free. That open heart sacrifice that could potentially alter families. Changing the seeds of time yet leaves its mark with just a mere medal for their imminent sacrifices.

I recently went to bat for a couple Legion members that I hold in very high esteem. These individuals work extremely hard to assist their fellow comrades. One person for reasons unknown other than a personal control has made these peoples' lives a nightmare. Bullying at any stage of life is sick. This type of person moves from day to day thinking only of their own wants, not a care in the world, treading on the ones who offer everything so openly to their fellowman. If there is any justice in this life, the self-centered who take advantage of their fellowman will find themselves wandering the desert of life trying to gain access to a utopia forever beyond their reach. This is not meant to be judgemental rather merely stating a fact. Some people seek out their own rewards in life and in this instance this is one.

I have a very strong feeling of a past military life. To sit and watch something as simple as an old war movie re-enacted but feel so very much a part of it. To think that you could express the next move or thought is eerie to say the least but I have been there. I know the pull to research such happenings is there for a reason. Do we all get these past life experiences flashing through our minds? Is it that some people get them more than others?

I returned to my first real base, to the aviation museum that has been established in the thirty five years since. I walked through the doors and recognized a person, I had not seen in at least forty years. What are the odds? We only said basic introductions and related to the time we knew each other, but what was the purpose of this chance meeting? I believe everything has a meaning, will this lead to another conclusion? Is this person going to tell another that we met and that is the person that has something to pass on to me? That is where my mind takes me. A chance conversation always has a purpose, what we do with it is another.

Any way it is viewed the seed has been planted to flourish in the generations to follow. This is a seed which carries the connections to so many previous generations, with overtones of environmental influences.

## Chapter Eleven

# Cremation

I recently drove by a crematorium and I seen dark smoke emanating from the chimney, I instantly had a brain flash to the holocaust and a tear ran down my cheek. I have no apparent connection to the holocaust that I know but somewhere in my past this pain was felt. I have no problem with cremation and that is my final wishes. I am so in tune with what I want in that respect I have designed and made my own urn. I have hand carved the design I wanted. Another task I don't have to leave to whoever takes care of me when my time comes. I have also designed my own headstone but haven't taken the steps to have it built. One common joke amongst the family is I am trying for the record books by having a plot in every province in Canada. My rebuttal is at least I own a little property to call my own.

When dad was dying and I knew his final wishes were never brought forward. It wasn't a subject other than he wanted to be cremated, that he would openly discuss. The day came we were all sitting at the kitchen table at the family's summer cabin. I knew his cremation wish but I also wanted the rest of the family to hear it with their own ears. With that out of the way, I took the next set to find out what cemetery plots were available and when the family was all together we went to the cemetery and walked the area not realizing at the time the plot he walked right to was adjacent to his parents. The task was done and dad walked that mile realizing when all was said and done he had a spot or placement that he took an active part in.

There are often difficult subjects that have to be address and if a person allows fear to prejudge the situation such as death to many decisions are made out of haste and sometimes end up very costly. In my dad's situation, it was a family guided into a family decision prior to a devastating outcome. Calmer heads did prevail prior to the ultimate time of grieving. I recently went back to see how his headstone had handled the winter. I realized there was an unclaimed spot two over from his which I earmarked for myself.

A topic that was seldom talked about in the family home is easily and openly talked about by all as the need requires it. Death is nothing to fear and we may as well, have our intensions known long before necessity dictates it. My oldest sister's first son died at a very early age from heart problems. They were not prepared for this to happen, nor was anyone else in the family. The arrangements they were talked into at that time never ever met their expectations. To this day it remains a problem. A cousin of ours, said at the time he would be there for him and he was. He died shortly after. I believe we know our time and many stories are known to substantiate that statement. The fact is whether we care to relate to it at the time or not.

We have experienced a lot more rain this spring than normal, and I have heard stories where burial plots are starting to bulge up from the various water levels experienced. My dad used to relate stories where he would be a pallbearer and coffins would be floating in the bottom of graves when they had graveside ceremonies. It was situations like this that confirmed the necessity to be cremated when the time comes. I believe it is easier for the family to address and accept when the time comes. Rather than viewing an expired body at a service an image that doesn't sit well at the best of times. With a service where the onlookers are more concerned over what our final garb worn was and how we looked as we left this earth. This is a crude description to express ones end but yet so true. To relate to a throwback from so many other life experiences only adds credence to an already difficult situation.

In my research with Genealogy, I of course walk a good many cemeteries looking for clues that will further tie the reference material together and in a good many older situations offer up a mere photo that the person even existed. I view some headstones knowing that the plot size could never accommodate the names expressed there within. With that also realizing that cremation has always not been a chosen preference either. This leads on to wonder if they were placed elsewhere and only covered with an annotation that they even existed. That has always been a bug-a-boo of mine that a person can go their whole life without so much as a mark to say they were here. To me an absolute waste, to live a complete life and poof gone, erased from the earth. To end up as a line in a church record or a numbered plot in the cemetery's archives, just doesn't make any sense. To be scattered to the wind, free from this life, very poetic in nature but again there needs to be some evidence that you walked this earth. If not for the person gone, rather for the possible generations to follow. That is a thought from a genealogist's perspective. These are questions that come to light with no answers. Where did they come from? Where did they go? The list goes on, and my father's side is a prime example I go nowhere fast on that side of the family. There is a key out there somewhere and I strive to find it someday otherwise it is a seed I will plant leaving enough clues for someone else to run with.

*Eyes Closed, Too Hear*

We need a window, a snapshot in time to help find the answer to our questions, so simple but true.

    I recently was told a story, where this person's grandmother died and her final request was her ashes were to be returned to her homeland. Shipping ashes at that time presented a problem, so the family researched what products could be sent. They came to the conclusion they could use cocoa. The ashes were mixed into cocoa and sent. A letter was sent under separate cover and never arrived until a week after the cocoa arrived. Also at this time in the hometown there was a wedding, needless to say this new treasured cocoa was used in conjunction with the festivities. I will leave the rest to ones imagination.

## Chapter Twelve

# Faults

Each family has their own vices, ours has been relatively blessed that drugs hasn't been a devastating problem. Alcohol and tobacco, we have dealt with through each generation. And tobacco is quickly disappearing. Alcohol is another topic.

I remember at the beginning of my military career one situation that marked a series of events that if done today would have warranted a nice cell with the key thrown away. I knocked out all my front teeth after a dare to ride a horse bareback coupled with several beer. Another time, my car was dirty and my buddy said come down here there is a real shallow spot in the river where we can wash it. No sooner said than done we drove in the river and the water was running into the car through the open windows it was so deep. Talk about a real sobering effect, cold too.

There was another time I had gone home to see the family. It was near my birthday so friends and neighbours gathered together and we went to a popular bar for that time to celebrate. My parents' best friends had just bought this spanking new car. First one they had in a long time. Long story short one of my buddies said he felt sick. He was told whatever he did not to get sick in the car; no sooner said than done he christened it. I don't know what all he ate because it seemed like he lost a week's worth of something. That story comes up at least once a year and it never loses it punch. My buddy died several years ago on the golf course, doing something he loved.

Another time. My cousins, a couple friends and I invited ourselves to a real old fashion Ukrainian wedding. Homebrew was ample and the wedding was wild. We headed home in my uncle's brand new car and on the way we decided to go to the lake for a swim. The hour was getting late, so we took the back road home. We all fell asleep as the car slowly followed the country road on its own. I remember opening my eyes as branches started slapping the side of the car. Then Bang. The biggest Poplar jumped out right in the middle of the car and planted itself well into the front grill and rad. Steam masked our stop and everyone awoke proclaiming the car was on fire. We had to walk back home, revising our story several times, getting more and more concerned as we got closer. Let's put it this way, it was very light when we walked in the yard. My uncle was not impressed, the car was fixed and the first road trip he took it on a deer jumped in front of him, same damage. All was forgiven; it had to be the car. How could we have two similar accidents back to back?

Auntie, dad's live-in babysitter was what we view today as a hoarder. She had this little room at the top of the stairs. You could barely walk into this room and to this marvel that the door even closed. Walking in this room as a child we were always told not to touch anything. Auntie would be on her bed, head wrapped in towels, clothes or something. She had clotheslines suspended above the bed and she would brush the white nylon socks out of the way to look at us. Everything was stacked up from the floor covering any visible spot. There could be anything from a part box of chocolates white with age; to a cold cup of tea separated with a surface film of something drinkable many days past. Hairpins and hairnets were everywhere, within hands reach, cards, papers, receipts, tickets, magazines and flyers discarded or put aside for a later read. Layers and layers of blankets and bedclothes mounded to cover her eccentrics.

After my dad's mother died and Auntie took over the whole house this accumulation also manifested. She died of an open cancer. There was so many of her day to day items were burnt without a second glance. Part way through the clean-up of her affairs it was realized she never used a bank for anything. Pinned to almost any new stored item was money, amounts beyond all beliefs. Part used laundry detergent boxes were stuffed with money. I don't know what the exact amount found was but more over it is also unknown the amount that was destroyed in the initial burning.

I have only met one other person like that, we had the task to help clean-up her trailer after her passing. After two hundred large garbage bags we didn't even put a dent in the accumulation removed. A lot of items never even seen the inside of a garbage bag they were carried straight to the awaiting trailer. To have pets in this atmosphere, words can't even describe, mold, rot, feces and dead accumulated hair to say the least. A lesson above all lessons, not to accumulate beyond our everyday needs. This is a lesson where we can't take it with us and others don't really see the same value with our treasures.

In my following of numerology I keep getting the repeat message to download all my unnecessary material items. To streamline my life, my direction has me on the move to fulfill my destiny. I haven't received the date of this happening but I am constantly being aimed east. Will this happen before I finish my book I don't know. I am going east shortly but is this going to satisfy my urge, I believe it is merely an awakening. The seed was planted and my destiny is outlined in the grains of sand on a tide-swept beach. To be followed or wiped clean if I don't heed my calling. To follow an alternate, etching which will ultimately draw me to the same conclusion. My life has always has been in search of something, I am close but not there. I now know I had to reach this point and live the pain I lived to attain my next calling. It is so hard to express to someone that hasn't been blessed with such a presence. To work towards opening my heart and seeking overall forgiveness for my mistakes has shed a whole new perspective to my purpose. We are not in as much control as we think we are. Our moulding is like we are toys of a higher power introducing us to situations of life to study the results. To bring us to the perfect conclusion in our wayward existence.

When we had our Family Reunion in 1992 we put out a family history book and a family recipe book. A letter was sent to each adult to submit a blurb about them, their family and a favourite recipe. The results were not fantastic rather normal for a family of our size. But one recipe still comes to mind, one that my father submitted.

*RJ Woodward*

## Dad's Rum Cake

- 1 or 2 quarts Rum
- 1 cup Butter
- 1 tsp. Sugar
- 2 large eggs
- 1cup dried fruit
- Baking powder
- 1 tsp. Soda
- Lemon juice
- Brown sugar
- Nuts

*Before you start, sample the Rum. Good isn't it?. Now go ahead. Select a large mixing bowl, measuring cup, etc. Check the rum again. It must be just right. To be sure the rum is of the highest quality, pour one level cup of rum into a glass and drink it down. Repeat.... With an electric mixer beat 1 cup of butter in a fluffy bowl. All 1 seaspoon of thugar and beat again. Meanwhile, make sure that the rum is of the finest quality. Try another cup. Open second quart if necessary. Add 2 arge leggs, 2 cups fried druit and beat til high. If dried fruit gets stuck in beaters just pry is loose with a drewscriver. Sample the rum again, checking for tonscisticity. Next, sift 3 cups of peper or salt ( it really doesn't matter). Next sift ½ pint of lemon juice. Fold in chopped butter and strain nuts. Add i bubblespoon of brown thugar, or whatever color you can find. Wix mel. Grease oven and turn cake pan to 350 gredees. Now pour the whole mess boven and ake. Check the rum again, and go to bed.*

My parents use to make homemade wine. My friend and I did taxidermy together, as we got older we used to sample this wine and top the bottles off with water. Dad would bring out a bottle and serve it always remarking "I don't know what we are doing wrong!! This stuff tastes weak". This went on for quite a considerable amount of time before they clued in. There was one gallon jug in particular, that was made from choke cherries. This jug had sat for years and dad kept saying he should throw it out because it sat for too long. We decided to test it, not disturbing the dust on the bottle we gave it a whirl, Wow was it good. We topped it off and it was still good. So I convinced dad he should try it before he got rid of it. What have you got to lose I said. I think that was when the light came on.

Homemade wine has also been a trying event. There were several batches that popped their corks always at the strangest hour of the night. Bringing the whole family to state of readiness wondering if WWIII was about to start. After the family moved to the new house, many eruptions took place under the kitchen counter till procedures we mastered. I was long from home by then so the procedure of watering down came to an abrupt halt another direct indicator that something was remiss while I was there.

I like to say we have a few moon people in our family tree. It seems as we get close to a full moon we can expect a few weird things to happen. As time has gone by, and we are all getting older we anticipate these situations to rear their ugly head yet another month. The bigger and brighter the full moon, the more intense the problems seem to be. The only thing that is a given is we only know of a couple that present these traits. For this we are thankful, we do watch each new generation for possible new additions. It is just another fault that comes with a larger family tree. One could say this fault is a level of bi-polar but the big problem is it has to be recognized in order to correct it. If you never do anything wrong and it is someone else's doing then for sure it will never be recognized. That is the mystery of faults that somewhere needs to be corrected.

When our thoughts reduce us to the level of other people's faults is it right or revenge? Because we should know better and they may not know what they have done. They may be too caught up in their lives to realize their own actions. All you can really feel is pity for them. Knowing that one day, they will be held accountable.

We all have been guilty of open mouth insert foot. Mouth is working before the brain turns on. Pick your statement there is hundreds of them. We say things that once they are out, can't be eaten very easy. They leave marks, they hurt and sometimes there is no call for the deluge of spew we have to fathom. But we do, sometimes we do it out of love, family or witness it happening to someone else. Anyway you look at it, it boils down to a learned behavioural issue, and we have learned this from a past experience. If we are guilty, recognize it and strive to remove it from your character. I always say "This can't be passed to another generation!!" and I truly believe this. Anything that I see that happens in the family and I don't like it I say the same thing. If I am to be remembered for anything that statement is one that can be quoted. That is a seed I would like to plant in every young mind for generations to come.

## Faults

*From our mouth we utter the words*

*It's your fault can't you see*

*It is your faults so why dice me.*

*So whose fault is it really?*

*When no one takes the blame*

*Whose fault is it if truthfully?*

*Someone needs to claim*

*The fault is mine I*

*I am the bigger person*

*I will assume this toll*

*Because I allowed it*

*To get far out of control.*

*Author Me*

## Chapter Thirteen

# Money Effects

I want it to be known, you can't buy love. Doesn't matter how much is put on the table it just won't cut it in the end. Money always comes at a price, sometimes a very heavy price. I have witnessed the best of families falling apart over a meagre sum of money. I have seen so many situations where a parent has said I will buy you this if you do that. Don't sell your soul and don't buy into it either. No one wins. I have seen families where the only conversation they have is about money and what they are going to buy next.

What are you teaching a child if everything rotates around money? What message can possibly come from it? It is a short term fix, nothing more nothing less.

My mother's dad had journals of everything, he could tell you where every penny was spent. What the weather was on any given day and what the temperature was several times a day. He recorded every time the car turned a wheel and where they went. Every day he would walk downtown for the mail and he would always carry a double brown paper shopping bag. If he got a new book or magazine he would put it between the layers of the shopping bags and sneak it into the house. It wasn't that my grandmother minded it was because so many times he told her they couldn't buy certain required items that she asked for. She would ask where the book or magazine came from and he would always say "Oh I had that for a long time. It was in the bookcase upstairs. It was only after one visit from my mother did she start setting money aside from her old age pension did she get to buy the things she wanted. Like a little deep freeze which they left with the house when they moved back West.

On that move I was still in the military and my uncle and I went down East packed everything up and I had to catch a military flight home. My uniform shoes were packed by mistake so I had to wear an old pair of my grandfather's. He always walked so that the shoes wore badly on the outside of the heel. Well my legs were so tired by the time I got home I couldn't walk straight for days and I was only flying not walking.

Isn't it ironic that this topic falls on the number thirteen, a number that so many have trouble with. I have always believed thirteen as my lucky number, having no problem with it and I totally look forward to Friday the $13^{th}$. We live beyond our means that appears to be a given, in today's society, I have lived through times when money was tight. So many today have no idea what it is like to butter toast with fat drippings or re-use a teabag till there is nothing left. In my dad's parents house only the ones working got to eat meat all the younger children had bread and gravy with their main course.

I have recently planned a trip with my youngest son to tour the east coast this summer, not to be outdone my estranged wife books a trip to the west coast and down to Los Cabos , Mexico. That gesture instantly made me feel my son has become a pawn in a game of chess. I have decided I will not play this game with a person's life and choose to opt out of this situation entirely. I am going to remove myself, even though my gesture initially came from the heart. I know that this thoughtless style of tug of war can only hurt my son. He is of the age that he can now form his own opinions and will eventually see through all this. We shall still take our trip, to penalize him for this action, is unfair. The price paid to negate an action of love meant to introduce a taste of his heritage. This was to be a snapshot into the past and a path to his future generations. If these trips were planned months apart-"OK" . To find out about this trip planned for merely a couple weeks later-"NO". There is no malice on my part, rather stating a fact.

As I stated before this mile is not mine to walk, it is the path that has been introduced as a quick fix and an avenue to further pain when the day of reckoning arrives. A closed heart can only feel pain, stimulated over and over through un-thoughtful actions. I pray this will be corrected in due time, that my son will not remain a victim of "stick with me and I will buy whatever you want syndrome"

I have repented for my negative ways and I have been rewarded or this in ways far beyond monetary gains. I know from this day forward my life will be guided and cared for, my needs will be met. The hurts I felt in the past will no longer cause pain and I can aspire to my future. I can give from the heart and not expect a return. Money is no longer the be-all end-all to my happiness. I will survive.

It took a long winding road to get to this spot. To share the pain experienced, not to absolve you from this pain rather to tell you there is a way through it. Open your heart and plant that seed be motivated to make change. The rewards are so bountiful when the heart is free to re-enforce your true destiny. The desire to help and share with others; the costs are so minuet and the benefits so plentiful. Don't let money consume you.

You see so many parents that live vicariously through their children doing the things they never did themselves.

The push, the control is so sickening, the stifled goals buried to make a drama queen or a star athlete. Where have all the moral values gone? The seeds we plant can only rot away the purest form of life, a child. The child, so easily moulded to form our next generations. The child if moulded wrong has the potential to become the next mass murderer or suicide bomber. What are we doing? What are we missing? I know we just can't see it.

    We are all taught about money at an early stage of our life. Some have it, some don't. As kids we were encouraged to raise our own spending money. When we were at the cabin we would catch and sell frogs for 25 cents a dozen to the fishermen that didn't have time to catch their own after work. It was a great business and carried us through each summer. Matter a fact there were people that would come back looking for the kids that sold frogs long after we left home. We didn't only catch frogs on one occasion we brought home a litter of shrews that didn't go over as well as expected. But we did.

    We all had our babysitting service also once we were of age to care for others. It is funny to run into the different people we cared for and merely remark how we used to babysit them when they were young. Some that looks as old as we do now. Time has a funny way of balancing the scale. We look at the parents that remain and realize we are now beyond the age when of what they were when we were babysitting their children.

> *"A little more persistence, a little more effort, and what seemed hopeless failure may turn to glorious success." - Elbert Hubbard*

> *"If you love wealth more than liberty, the tranquility of servitude better than the*

*animating contest of freedom, depart from us in peace. We ask not your counsel nor your arms. Crouch down and lick the hand that feeds you. May your chains rest lightly upon you and may posterity forget that you were our countrymen."* - Samuel Adams

*"I am absolutely convinced that no wealth in the world can help humanity forward, even in the hands of the most devoted worker. The example of great and pure individuals is the only thing that can lead us to noble thoughts and deeds. Money only appeal of self-indulgence."* - Albert Einstein

## Chapter Fourteen

# Momentous Events

I remember in 1963 when the president was shot, I was working in the local confectionary store. I was filling an order for a soft ice cream cone, the announcement came on the TV, I stood there in disbelief as this cone got bigger and bigger. There were so many people; on that day frozen in time, not knowing which way to turn. I later found through my genealogy that his family blends into our family tree. Once again I believe for a moment I was touched by a kindred spirit.

Our family tree is graced with some very dignified people. Our family tree has Royalty, Dignitaries, Movie stars and Political figures each with a story of their own; each with their own mile and seeds to plant. What I enjoy the most is the struggles of the everyday people to leave their mark on the world. The mark that has the potential to stand the test of time. A story, as pure and simple as the first day it was told, that moves through history like a floating leaf.

I remember in awe as the "King of Rock N' Roll" appeared on TV for the first time. His shake rattle and rock took us all to a world we had never seen before. Clearing the way for the English four and the Wanna-Be's. Those were all moments in history, during the birth of TV that kids could never relate to today. So many momentous things have happened to clear the way for modern technology. Each generation views their changes as the best. To remember all the tubes and knobs too make our technology work now is like a postage stamp in our hand a chip, a Bluetooth, a mere thought constantly changing bringing us further into the future. These seeds that were planted shall move generations to come. The scrolls, the records, the databases to the future, our life really needs to simplify to bring back the ultimate values. The values that have too fuse with our modern times.

    My mother and her brother worked for dad's brother in his bakery. Mom's parents had gone to Nova Scotia for a couple weeks. Just prior to their return dad's brother took it on himself to ensure the two were ready for their parents return. He took my uncle and put him in the big pot sink and scrubbed him down with a pot brush to ensure he was clean. My mother had developed a boil on one hand so he took a hot pop bottle and drew the core out as the bottle cooled. By the time the grandparents arrived everything was back shipshape. Except for the kitchen sink, the housekeeper had poured bacon grease down the sink everyday while they were gone and plugged things pretty solid.

    Do we actually see everything we are meant to see? Are we only seeing what we choose to see? I believe we are missing so many momentous events because our hearts aren't programmed to stop and actually smell the roses. We need to adjust all our sense to witness and appreciate the beauty of the finer things in life. A baby's first step, a child's first pet, a teenager's first date whatever your mind can see as a momentous occasion that should be treasured.

    My mother told me about a wedding her, my sisters and their families went to just recently. The whole day it rained. The wedding service itself was beautiful but once they got to the hall afterwards everything turned into a nightmare.

The meal was 1 ½ hours late after an eventful happy hour. There were about 320 guests and after about 80 were served the entire staff walked out including the bartenders who took with them all the cash from the bar. At that point key friends stepped up to the plate and carried the function through. Meals were served and people volunteered to run the bar. To top it all off the photographer was called away to an emergency and another guest volunteered to take pictures. I said well the way today's society is going the Good Lord wants to see if you are up to the challenge right from the get go. He puts you through a real test and if you can handle the situation then you are good for the long haul.

Every time I find another piece to the puzzle that pulls our family tree into a stronger unity I feel this is another momentous event for the family. When one compares the anatomy of a tree the upper branch network can only compare to the root maze hidden beneath it. The foundation, the same hold true with a family if the foundation isn't strong the fibre that holds it all together slowly fragments and it falls apart. For me the strongest tree and most vibrant is the mighty oak, its leaves are so green and its seed are so perfect. That strength runs deep in my moral makeup and gives me drive to last just as the oak outlasts almost any adversity. If that isn't momentous nothing is and another seed is planted for someone to pickup and carry on.

My hometown has just completed another homecoming celebration. I attended this event, taking in a few of the venues seeing people I hadn't seen for in some cases up to 46 years. Listening to stories of the various paths that lives were taken to come to the point where we had the chance encounter to meet again. For some life hasn't been totally fair to them, they haven't aged as well as others. Their hidden stories reveal the good and bad times of their lives. Coming to the total realization that time has marched by and it is now time to question what is left for future generations. Many realizing our throwaway society has also touched them in a way that can have nothing but an adverse effect if drastic changes aren't made. The life lessons learned can only be their seeds planted for future generations. To feel these common thoughts only re-enforces the beliefs I already carry.

    One thing that has been passed from one generation to the next is the allergy to wasps. My mother is to the point where any wasp bite could be her last, yet she never carries her medication. My nephew has acquired the same trait. One day, he said "Great grandma if we both get bit by a wasp what will we do? Mom always says you get the first needle, I have lived my life!"

> *"A happy marriage is a long conversation which always seems too short."*
> *- Andre Maurois*

## Chapter Fifteen

# Epiphanies

As our family was getting larger, I was given the opportunity to make my own bedroom in the basement. Close to the homemade wine, joke. I went to the local grocery store and dragged home a bunch of apple box layers. They were purple and reminded me of little boobies, I was at that age. I installed all these liners on the ceiling of my room and marvelled at them through my teen years. The house was sold and a couple years ago my sister had the opportunity to go through the old place to see if it had changed. She went into the basement and my ceiling was still there. Color had changed but it stood the test of time. A symbol of a childhood adventure strange as it may seem. This is one which touched other people as they took their turns living in that house. I wonder what their first impression was when they seen that ceiling.

Some seeds that were planted have taken on the adverse effect. My mother's dad had keys, he had locks for everything. His pocket bulged from so many keys, he would double lock every door then go back several times to ensure the door was locked There was times we would get several miles away and he would have to go back and check his locks. On the other hand is my mother, thankfully she lives in a very small town. She very seldom locks anything, you can find her car almost anywhere with keys in the ignition and it is extremely rare to find her doors locked. Her guardian angel really has to be on overtime, keeping her from harm's way. Mom biggest concern is if she left the coffee pot on, she double checks hers every time she goes out. This comes from one event when my parents went out of town to visit my sister a nagging thought gave her the feeling she forgot something. It finally dawned on her what it was, so she phoned her neighbour to go check. Sure enough the pot had cooked dry and was well on its way to melting into the countertop.

There was this one time, when my mother first came to stay at my dad's parents' home. She was introduced to the fact if she had to go to the bathroom at night she would have to use a chamber pot located under the bed. Being somewhat embarrassed to use it the first time she mustered up enough courage and went. In the process the thunder mug cracked in half and the contents ran though the floor and dripped off the light on to my grandparents' bed. This was not the nicest introduction to the family but it has been a story that has survived generations to still be retold on occasion.

I recently had a conversation with my older sister about how we have at times harboured the feelings that our children may have not been accepted in the same light as others in the family. Is that insecurity or a fact? Does it have a bearing on the geographical location of their upbringing over other members of the family? One would like to think that. Or is it just the plain truth of starting a family so early in life we hadn't matured enough to address it effectively. I think the later has a strong bearing on it, the older kids in our family all left home early. We started our own lives and did what we thought was best for that time. The need to still be ever so present in our children's lives is to day's by-product. We don't want history to repeat itself yet again. The thing is can we stop it? Or induce yet another problem. To change the path of destiny so engrained in us. The choice becomes our, we get to plant the next seed.

After a recent early talk with a friend, I feel asleep and went into a dream within a dream. I have stated before I go to sleep I give thanks for recent things that have influenced my life. One thought of thanks was for the guidance and direction received in writing this book. In my dream. I see this page of writing it is quite blurry and it is floating through the air. As this page gets closer it is what I had just done in written form. It reads; I placed my phone on my pillow and put my head on top to hold it there, my <u>Eyes Closed too Hear</u> blinking boldly on the page. I read further and another statement <u>Learning to Love</u> was also boldly blinking. Reading on <u>A Gift</u> this went on to others <u>My Angel</u> being one. I woke with tears running down my cheeks.

Remarkable I had just received a subliminal message about my book. Is this where the title came from? Was it something as simple as this? Was "Learning to Love" a sequel or a book within a book? For a few days I was struggling with the direction I wanted to take. Because of this there were a dozen chapter titles I couldn't put my finger on. I had several ideas on which way I should head. Then the seed was planted. The seed was in my dreams. This is absolutely remarkable and the guidance placed before is almost beyond belief. I am not going to question the revelation I have felt, I am going to accept this with thanks on my future prayers to come. My faith from this epiphany has taken on stronger meaning that we all have a destiny if with an open heart we behold.

I now feel I am not finished, there is more direction to come. My hand is merely the instrument to pass this message on. Too make it sound as simple as a message that only an open heart can deal with anything. To keep us all positive with our purpose in life and strive to meet through the will so deep within us placed there by our maker.

How many can wake up one morning and say this is the day I am going to start "_____". It could be absolutely anything from losing weight to exercising. They are going to make a change in their life. What happened since going to bed and waking up the next morning? What makes us so compiled to follow through with out epiphany? Then what makes others quit several times before they succeed? Was it a statement they heard subliminally in the middle of the night? The questions are endless, the follow through is another thing. I always said I would know the day I was going to retire from the military. One morning I got up and did just that. I knew what I was doing. I wasn't mad. I just knew my time had come.

I have seen people so afraid to pull their hand from the mix that once forced to retire, die weeks later. I have never seen or met a person that was so indispensable that when they pulled their hand from a pail of water they left a hole. Yet there are so many that live their lives like they had that capability. How shallow are we to think at that level. One thing for sure, the heart really hasn't opened to enjoy the finer things in life.

> "The weaker the argument, the stronger the words".

> "The future you shall know when it has come; before then, forget it." - Aeschylus

I have come to realize that in my quest to find the purpose of life, i have been drawn to one conclusion. We must live life to its simplest form to love, with respect and cherish every living being. I have also stated this in another chapter but if we accept this life is really not that complicated. We make the choices for the ultimate changes and from these I believe we as humans have really screwed up.

I have noticed with my website, the harder I promote living green, the more social interplay comes into play. Everyone has a cause they want you to join or support but it all comes back to the same thought. We need to remove the lust of hate, murder, kill and destroy from our day to day life. Easier said than done, but it is true, without those type of thoughts we could all live in harmony. Take for example; How can one hate another that they have never met because of a mere statement, thought or action? They could have been having a bad day or as in some of our well known leaders "The mouth is in gear before the brain" and they spend the rest of their political career trying to correct that one slip. We expend far too much energy trying to identify the faults in others.

To hate, to me is such a harsh statement. This is one that really needs to be looked at by everyone. We as humans have screwed up and no matter how we look at it; our day is coming to atone to our actions. I do not believe everyone will have to suffer through the actions of others but a good many will. We are on that type of threshold right now, the choices we make; the seeds we plant will have a definite bearing on the end outcome. That simple, pay me now or pay me later. The choice is yours. To me just don't cry over your choice, I have made mine and want to share.

> *"The point in history at which we stand is full of promise and danger. The world will either move forward toward unity and widely shared prosperity - or it will move apart."*
> *- Franklin D. Roosevelt*

## Chapter Sixteen

# Kids in the Hood

The kid next door we played together, like it seemed forever in the early years. But amazingly enough we had drifted apart by the age of say eleven. His thoughts and ideals had taken him down a far different path than mine. He still wanted to hang out but his moods really didn't fit my nature. Any way one time, in his backyard we were playing with firecrackers. This one time the fuse was lit, a larger can like a jam or coffee can was put on top and he stood on the can to feel the whomp. Wrong, It went off and blew a hole in his shoe, so ended those antics. Another lesson learned, the hard way, thankfully he wasn't injured.

We had this family that lived kitty-corner from us. I would like to say there were only three kids but I just can't remember. Two boys and a girl. Anyway they were always different, lots of fun but different. Trouble came in capital letters with them. They had an old grandmother living with them, she would start bawling them out for something and they would tie her to a chair and put her in the garage. Crazy stuff like that. One day the younger boy had aches in his foot so he went in the house and taped two aspirins to his foot. Another time he was chasing me on his bike and I put a stick through the front wheel and he flew over the handlebars into the tall grass. Un-scathed, to live yet another disastrous adventure.

*Eyes Closed, Too Hear*

As young kids, we loved to play marbles; we lived a few doors down from the public school so we went there to play on the basketball court. We were the envy of a lot of the kids because we always had "Steelies" the ball bearings from worn out bearings at the bakery. One day this bigger kid and I mean bigger kid grabbed me and took me by the ankles and shook all the marbles out of my pockets and ran off with them. Today he would be viewed as a bully and corrective action would have been taken. Back then nobody said anything, his size and meanest carried through to High School where he took the French teacher and held him out the school window because he didn't want to learn French.

I remember as a kid so many things were done with a team of horses and a wagon. Garbage collection, milk delivery and freight were to name a few. The streets would have piles of horse buns everywhere and in the winter when frozen made ideal hockey pucks. On this one occasion, I picked up one of these frozen lumps and threw it at this passing wagon hoping to spook the horses. This object being frozen skipped across the ground and bounced up on this passing car's windshield. The car stops and we took off in all direction thinking we might get caught.

Speaking of winter, we would hitch a ride on passing cars by ducking down and skiing on their back bumpers. The streets weren't paved back then so sudden stops and potholes really added to the challenge. If caught the driver would stop and shake their fist at us. We would laugh and take off. Those types of things done today would really cause a problem mind you cars now are faster and with streamlining there are fewer things to grab onto.

The local playground was our stomping grounds; the swings are gathering spot. This playground was called "The Triangle" we would hang out there till dark that was our cut-off time    and we had to be home. Heaven forbid if we were late no excuse was accepted. Rules were rules." But" was never, ever accepted.

We also had a sledding hill we used to all gather at in the winter. We would slide on absolutely anything. A piece of cardboard was a common sight. A wooden toboggan or a metal -runner sled were seen all over this hill. Safety was never a concern, a toque, a scarf, a pair of mitts, a warm parka and boots then gone for the afternoon.

One sports day in school, I would like to think either Grade V or VI on a dare I at earthworm to impress this girl. My older sisters to this day will drop that back into the conversation. If we were to be held accountable for everything we have done in our younger years, many of us wouldn't see the light of day. And for sure we wouldn't be in too big a hurry to encourage others to walk in our shoes. Some of us are just naturals at doing this type of thing. It leaves a lot of room for others to aspire to.

We had a hedge of Caraganas, which we used as our fort or hiding place. We would eat the yellow flowers as these shrubs would come into bloom and make whistles from the pods when they went to seed. These were old bushes and they offered up a few good scratches also. The imagination was our playground and we could do almost anything there.

These are seeds worth passing on. Seeds that is worth more than any money spent today on lavish equipment to stand-out on a hill. Life was rather simple then, we didn't have to out-do our friends with stuff our parents couldn't afford. Something as simple as a hula-hoop has kept generations entertained, it contains a challenge, it is physical, capable to be done by all age groups. Take this seed and think about it very seriously. What can't you afford to pass on? Keep it simple and the rewards will be great.

As teens, Halloween in our hometown was an event that for the mercy of all that is pure and glorious many of us were fortunate to survive. We would all head off with pure innocence, promising not to get into any trouble. That would change at the first corner, out would come the rotten eggs and bags of poop. We would egg the non-partakers' windows or put a burning bag of poop on their step and depart with a quick knock. Looking at it today we are lucky we never burnt down any homes in the process. On time we quietly piled the wood pile in front of the door and knocked on the door with a stick, waiting for the angry response.

The ultimate of Halloween pranks was to tip over the outdoor shanties. It was a dirty job but someone had to do it. As we got older they were harder to find. One that stands out in my mind was when the owner of this one outhouse moved it forward for the hallowed event. Being after dark we ran up to push it over and the joke was on us we got introduced to the dirty side of the hole. Another time we were introduced to rock salt when the owner was inside and shot at us from the then exposed toilet hole. Those were the days. We kept the local police force hopping; one time we took a black spray can of paint and painted the headlights of the parked cruisers. In our later years, things had really changed; kids were rolling old tractor tires out on the street and setting them ablaze. That was one prank we never took part in and was probably for the best.

In high school one of the teachers had a Volkswagen car and we stuffed it right full of hay during a graduation festivity. It was these little things that marked our transition into young adults, things those years later we would frown on by the next generation's actions. We were afforded the knowledge, our parents already had. It was a time to confess and to find out what they really knew.

When my stepson was young and walking to school, he had to walk past a local gas station. This one day things got away on him and he had a bit of an accident in his pants. His mother, my second wife, had gone to the school to help out this day. She is walking by each of the student's desks to see if they needed help, when she happens along the stepson; the telltale aroma caught her instantly. She asked him if he had a problem and he said he brushed against the gas station's pumps. Saying nothing she hurried home to get a change of clothes because he didn't want the other kids to know. All was corrected rather quickly but the story has continued on all these years later. Merely referring to Fas-Gas does it for him.

I had a similar situation happen to me when I was in school. Every morning just before lunch break the kid that sat in front of me filled his pants like clockwork. This happened most of the one year, can't figure out how after doing it the first couple times, he didn't just make it known he had to go. If it was me I would have taken the strap, rather than sit in my one excrement because it was too close to lunch to go the washroom. Those were different times, but the punishment to me would still have been better.

We all have accidents at one time or other in our lives. A tinkle from laughing too hard, letting a little gas slip that turns out more solid than gas. Those all add to life's most embarrassing moments. Same as getting sick, if it has to come out it doesn't matter where you put your hand it is going to spray around it. Or one could be sitting at a bar and there just aren't enough glasses on the table to fill because you got sick to fast to make it to the washroom. Oh life's special moments. The wastebasket can be right by the bed and you miss it by inches, this stuff happens. We don't have too much choice when and where we get sick and the combination sickness and runs, detail a whole different set of life skills on which to address first. To crack a smile at the mere though is probably as far as I will take this at this time.

On the same token, having one bathroom has its own series of stories when you have a house full of people. No matter what plans are in place inevitably someone will always get caught either needing to go or in the shower. Where the tap is turned on to freeze or scald them out. No paper, no towel seen it all. Curtain pulled for a quick relief, the flush and the proverbial "Oops, Sorry" and the shear panic in the shower. Words can't express that instant feeling that passes through each mind when this happens. At least today there are systems available to safeguard us from the total hot to total cold experience. The single bathroom can't always be addressed so easily.

Lego, has been the toy of choice for the last generations, it amuses young equally. It is limited only by the imagination of the person playing with it. I often think back to what we had to play with when I was young, the good old tinker toy building blocks. These blocks are still available, at a far greater price. Yet the Lego blocks have evolved to almost anything your mind can create.

During our recent homecoming celebrations I was fortunate enough to run into several other kids from the hood. One story related was about us playing softball in the neighbour's yard and we put the ball through their window. A couple parents had to step up and replace the window, dad being one and needless to say our ball playing days moved to the schoolyard after that. From this story another family friend related a story how my father's older brother loved to play two bag ball and whenever it was his turn at bat, he remained up to bat hitting the ball out of the park every time and no one else had a chance to get up to bat. Stories were told of this uncle that I had never heard before, his gentle, kind nature made him very popular in this small community. He left his mark and his influence is still present all these years later. A life taken early by a war he felt obligated to be part of.

    There are not too many kids that can't relate to a time in their life when they have played in the rain. To watch the sky turn black and have the sky light with lightning. Putting on rubber boots and attacking the various puddles after a storm was the attraction for every child. Running with make shift raincoats and fancy print umbrellas chasing the pooling water as it flowed down the street. Taking a stick or a piece of wood to make a little boat stimulated the young creative mind. The real challenge for every child was to see how high the water could rise on their boots before it flowed over the top and if you were really creative mud was the next event that could be entertained. If you were really lucky the suction would pull the boot off as you tried to pull away. Today, kids don't really experience these experiences; they play with their electronic toys with limited communication to the outside world.

## Kids in the Hood

Oh when we were kids, we didn't care

We lived our lives without much to spare.

We could take on the world,

And conquer our foes,

With a stick, a rope and heaven knows.

We handled life as best we could,

With next to no money, not understood

Yet today we need the best or we don't play.

Times have changed, now we have to pay

Kids in the hood need to learn

The respect they command

They have to earn.

                                      Author me

*"A child's understanding can often reveal things that the scientific and illuminated mind will seldom see." ~ Thomas E. Mails*

CHAPTER SEVENTEEN

# Keepsakes

My dad's mother had a china cabinet just off the dining room. There were only two items that caught our eye and kept us amused as kids. One was a plastic red donkey whose tail and head moved up and down. It probably popped cigarettes out its butt at one time but we would rush in to play with it when we visited. The other item was a snow globe with a Mountie in it; we had to really handle it with care for fear that if we ever broke it we would never hear the end of it. The donkey was always the first choice because we just couldn't hurt it.

Every generation comes with its keepsakes; these are the items that bond us with the past a realistic item that resembles the planted seed in the open heart. It could be absolutely anything and the value in the holders mind is priceless.

I have witnessed some real head shakers when dealing with keepsakes. My first wife's grandmother died and members of the family went in and took the light switch covers off the wall. They were plain old light switch covers less than a quarter in any hardware store.

On mom's side of the family the family china was passed down. Each female member seemed to take on their favourite pattern and from there the tradition grew. Some of these patterns were discontinued which made it hard to replace or add on to. The monetary value of these treasures is far beyond belief which once the tradition is broken it will carry on no more. The seed planted will stay dormant until a person finds the inspiration to nurture it and make it grow once again.

One time I gave my first wife a crystal oyster shell with a pearl in it and told her "Like a pearl where no two are the same that she was also one of a kind". She never got the full meaning of that statement. When she passed, I gave it to my mother as a remembrance of her and to this day it can still be seen mixed in with her keepsakes. We all take different meanings from items and someday someone will have to ask where the crystal shell came from as it is passed on as a start to their remembrance.

My mom's mother had recipes for all occasions. One of my favourites was her cheese biscuits and that has been my keepsake from her. They are so quick and easy to make. They help complete a homemade soup every time.

## Cheese Biscuits

- ½ or ¾ cup Grated cheese
- 2 cups flour
- 5 tsp. Baking powder
- 1 tsp. Salt
- 5 tbspn. Butter
- 7/8 cup milk

*Blend flour, baking powder, salt and butter. Add cheese and mix well. Add milk and rollout to about ¾ inch layer on a floured board or countertop. Take a glass about 2 inches in diameter pressing out circles until dough is used up. Bake in very hot oven for 10 -12 minutes watching they don't burn on bottoms.*

My keepsake that I want to pass down and share is my family tree. This has been a labour of love, through countless hours of research to find for future generations a link into their history. The stories are endless; you can find anywhere, the challenge to pass them on is part of dream. This is one of the seeds I want to leave behind.

Another point is everything we do have been so humanized filled with prejudice and judgement. The humanized keepsake is one that should fall by the wayside like talking behind someone's back. There is only on true statement to go with that and it is "If you are talking behind my back you are in a fantastic position to kiss my protruded posterior."

Keepsakes are something that is personal, that is what makes them keepsakes, not everyone carries the same interest. They can have a positive effect or a negative. I would like to think the keepsakes we cherish are not material items rather the positive moments that have touched us in a special way.

I recently saw a posting on Facebook where this woman was trying to record her mother's stories and the comments that followed we really not what she would have expected. I thought to myself "How can some people be so selfish to dash another person's desire to treasure her keepsakes close of her mother?" Is that not what I am doing in another form? I never got involved with the dialogue even though it bothered me.

I have witnessed how the younger family members so love stories of the past. It is their keepsakes, to pass on when their time comes. These are the ones I want to pass on and stimulate others to remember. Every action can become someone else's keepsake, trust me on that one. Receive this with an open heart and you will never erase the special ones from your mind. A seed planted as a keepsake like a mustard seed encapsulated in a necklace to hang in splendour till the end of our time.

My young nephew loves stories; he sits in marvel taking them all in. He never gets bored with them; my mother recently had the opportunity to babysit him. She related to him that I was writing a book about so many different stories he would like. He immediately asked if she could read it to him. She told him she didn't have a copy, and he said that was ok he could print one off on the computer. It makes me feel quite special to think that someone so young might find pleasure in some of my writings.

> *I admire him, I frankly confess it; and when his time is come I shall buy a piece of the rope for a keepsake - Mark Twain*

*RJ Woodward*

## Life's Treasures

Too clutch, to hold, to cherish dear

The keepsakes we keep so near.

To some these may seem like material things

But memories these items bring.

Why do we hold on to things so dear?

For the memories needed are in our heart

No one can tear them apart.

They are filled with love

Only time will take away the treasures

We no longer need.

The memories for when our days are done

Will too pass and be replaced

As someone else's treasure.

Author - me

## Chapter Eighteen

# Horoscopes

I am a Leo. I follow my horoscope religiously. I read it first thing every day. M y horoscope gives me a different perspective on life. It doesn't control my life rather it guides my life. What makes me a Leo? We are colourful, self assured, outgoing, impulsive and expansive. A Leo is authorative and affectionate. We expect praise and look to give praise.

I am to the point where I think a Taurus is my kryptonite. I seem to be drawn to them until I get gored a couple times. My wives both fell under the sign of Taurus and it is very evident throughout our family tree. I believe a Taurus should go with a Taurus because they do get some perverse pleasure out of butting heads. I have one sister that falls under that sign and she also finds difficulty with many of the family. I just find they have a different way in dealing with things that many don't understand. They are practical, stubborn, slow and deliberate. They have a natural interest in money and like to prove their worth.

If the wind blows a door shut it doesn't mean it was slammed in your face. There are alternatives and they have to be entertained. You have to love them though; if you can reach the heart and it is receptive they do have great qualities.

My two older sons are Aquarians. Similar traits, but different directions. They are both achievers in their own right. Aquarians are modern, progressive, diplomatic and humanitarian. They are also strong willed and inventive.

My mother and brother in law are both Pisces they are emotional, ultra sensitive, easy going, self sacrificing, understanding and sociable.

Now if you take a Virgo they are shy and prefer working behind the scenes. They are intellectual, critical, fussy, shrewd and have teaching abilities. They also lack confidence and need reassurance. A good counter balance for a Leo if they are diplomatic and allow the Leo to appear in charge.

Dad was a Libra. Libra's are fair and just, they try to maintain a proper balance. They are artistic, level headed, sympathetic, perceptive and generous.

You can see the range of personalities already expressed just by identifying different horoscopes. Then when they are blended with another sign, things can really get exciting. There are a few more yet to outlined. I like to deal in the positive so anything detailed so far are the positive attributes. The potential to have an open heart exists in every sign and should never be viewed any different.

Aries are quick, daring, self assertive and full of spunk. They are intelligent, energetic, and very impatient. They have lots of energy.

I have a couple sisters that are Capricorns honest, practical, ambitious, business like and careful. They are determined, dependable and maybe interested in collecting antiques.

Gemini, jack of all trades, highly adaptable, likes change and variety. They are restless and clever with their hands.

Cancer, emotional, intuitive, sympathetic and moody. They enjoy shopping and visiting friends. Have a interest in politics

Scorpio, intense, strong willed, determined, secretive. Nothing escapes their attention. They let tensions build to an exploding point. Deep thinkers and love a good fight. My second oldest sister is one.

Sagittarius, nervous energy, very optimistic, overlooks details, warm and friendly. They love to talk and travel and are outspoken. My youngest sister is one.

Throughout this book you will find reference to an influence to my guardian angels. One of course is my guardian angel for astrology but under this one there are others such as the angel of August, the angel of Leo and the angel of Saturday all playing a key factor in the guiding me to be me. Each one of these angels give me the strength and courage to move forward to my destiny. I have mentioned in this book where I know I am being guided each one of these influences form part of my inner being. We are not an entity on to our own as much as we think we are. With an open heart each one of these influences steer us along our destined path. Without the belief and knowledge to call upon we flounder along asking through greed for a direction to money and material things, lusting for a quick pleasure and wondering why it can't last a lifetime. Our needs will be met if we ask for the right things. Because of the influences set before us, waiting to be called on an support us in their enveloping wings.

Like horoscopes, I believe another influence that comes into play with our lives is biorhythms. The theory of biorhythms claims that one's life is affected by rhythmic biological cycles, and seeks to make predictions regarding these cycles and the personal ease of carrying out tasks related to the cycles. These inherent rhythms are said to control or initiate various biological processes and are classically composed of three cyclic rhythms that are said to govern human behaviour and demonstrate innate periodicity in natural physiological change: the physical, the emotional, and the intellectual (or mental) cycles. Others claim there are additional rhythms, some of which may be combinations of the three primary cycles.

There was a period of time when I used to make out my biorhythms faithfully. I got away from them but still believe they have an influence. I find with the desire to find myself and my purpose to life, each one of these influences plays a key part to identifying what comes into play.

> *"A physician without a knowledge of astrology has no right to call himself a physician ... There is one common flow, one common breathing, all things are in sympathy."*
>
> *Hippocrates*

## Chapter Nineteen

# Unconditional Love

I have read many articles on unconditional love and basically it is viewed as a powerful energy that lifts us through the most difficult times. This love requires dedication and intent to allow this energy to enter our daily lives.
As I pointed out before this love has to start with ourselves, for without first loving ourselves we cannot understand what true love can really be.

Forgiveness has to take place to remove the grudges from the past. This act opens the heart to better deal with the future. There is one rule of thumb you can't change a person unless they want to so learn to accept them for who they are. The next rule is if you want someone to change you are quite often the one with the problem in the first place. Are we so great that we want everyone to be in our likeness? I think the last one to make that request was in the heavens above and there has been a good many generations of people that have skirted around that issue. To live in a likeness is one thing but too clone is yet another.

Once you have an open heart it is no longer vulnerable and has no preset expectations or limits. The last point and probably the most important be yourself don't be what others expect you to be this stifles your respect for yourself.

Now take that seed and plant it, let it multiply and nourish for the betterment of mankind.

We are an entity on to our own, without our own pride and love there is no way you can command it for long from someone else. People will eventually see through. Without a strong foundation the temple crumbles and the heart sours. Lies are the worst to deal with because one leads to others which erodes the very cement that holds all together. Once caught in a lie the chances of getting caught just common.

Some levels of pain one endures to maintain happiness within their families is another example of real unconditional love. Families that have been torn apart by death, divorce and separation. There will always be one that will wear the hurt the deepest. The one with the purest heart. The one that gets to pick up all the pieces. To salvage what remnants that are left and carry on. We have all seen these people. We all know one but can we feel what they have gone through? Not many can.

I look forward to the day when I can be truly judged for what I have done here on earth. To know the love I have carried for my fellowman was moulded into the best person I could be. To know the people I touched in my life were given the best I could offer. To know that if have achieved forgiveness for any person I may have done wrong intentionally or not. That would be a fantastic gift of unconditional love. The reward for working to make life better for every person that had an influence in your life. What more could a person ask for. Then for sure a seed of unconditional love will have been passed on.

*A little bit of love can be*
*Like sunshine after rain,*
*And cause someone to realize*
*That life is not in vain.*
*We never know how very much*
*A bit of love can do;*
*And as we cheer another's heart,*
*Our own gets lighter too.*

- *Author Unknown*

Under the influence of the guardian angel for the tree of life, many factors dealing with love and its issues are addressed. This guidance comes from the crown of the tree to the root. Its influences are felt in the seed to its rebirth. Under the direction and guidance of this guardian angel I have been compelled to refer to the seed as the knowledge passé through a rebirth. Every point being made is under the guidance and influence of something away beyond me as an individual alone. I am moved to express my point away beyond what I thought was within my own understanding or comprehension. To this end the outside force can only be attributed to a guidance sent to you through a guardian angel. Everything I am exposed to on a day to day basis can now spin back to a line or topic in this book. I find I constantly refer to it being in my book. I can't believe this magnitude of coincidences.

*Patience in the present, faith in the future, and joy in the doing." - George Perera*

## Chapter Twenty

# The Draw

As I have stated throughout my book I am being drawn to the east coast I don't know why it so strong but it is there. My mother's father had the same type of pull when they went to Nova Scotia to retire. It was we the family that through constant urgings brought them back to the west. I never felt my grandfather had an influence on me in that respect. But is it really his thoughts that have influenced me or seeds planted by his forefathers. My grandfather always said his family came from Wales, through modern technology I have disproved his belief and found his ancestors come from Massachusetts. I can trace them back for many generations till the lineage stops. This drawing I feel takes me to this area. Is there something I have to do there? Is there someone I must find? What is the logic to this seed that is planted in my heart? I have a trip planned there next month but last night I realized that wasn't enough. I was researching places I would like to see while I am there with my youngest son. The drawing is so strong to be there now that I have booked a flight to Boston for next week. What can make us, move on such impulses? Will my inner desires be answered? So many questions and no answers.

This impulse is so strong I find I wake out of a deep sleep and feel the need to add my thoughts to this book. I am driven to share this feeling, to state that our lives have a definite predetermined purpose. I always thought I would be taking this trip with my second wife but the closer I get to my calling I now know she was never meant to walk this mile. In my visions this is now my mile and my mile alone. What I have to do now must be accomplished before I even proceed there with my son.

I could take this a step forward; in my followings of numerology, astrology and tarot readings I am being further guided to reduce my personal possessions in preparation of my travels. I am told I will meet a person from a French lineage and this person's spirituality shall take me to a place that I have been searching for all my life. Is this fate? Is it karma? One thing I do know it isn't a figment of my imagination. It has been to real too long. Everything of late I have set up as temporary, I have tried to establish a more solid footing in my current status. Each time I do something, I automatically move to a temporary mode because my destiny is not where I am. Where the drive becomes stronger to look east; I feel I am getting subliminal messages from my heart. Messages that each day take on a stronger direction.

We have the power to make decisions good, bad or indifferent, that's what makes us human. I have seen my father's life of regret over his choice of vocation even though he had a definite input later in life.

There is a reason why I must meet this person in my prophecies, there is something that has to happen. A seed must be planted, a seed that may influence generations to come. I believe my heart had to be open prior to discovering the full purpose of my predestined path. This drawing knows no boundaries, it knows no borders it is almost divine. My energies are needed to fulfill this direction.

I look for a meaning to everything I do, see and find. I believe this is all part of life's puzzle each piece adds to another to form our jigsaw of life. It is then layered in with the people we are exposed with and so on. The maze we create is all predestined and the challenge we have in our life is to find the key pieces that helps bring our puzzle together. Like with any puzzle the outside edges are essential and very easy to find it is the complex pieces that cause the many delays to move ahead in our life. To be drawn in a certain direction can totally take one off the easy path, it maybe a perceived direction that requires key components to be in place like a puzzle before the whole picture actually takes shape. One key piece that ties everything together.

Have you ever done a large multi-piece puzzle, looked at it forever not finding the piece you want? Then someone will walk right up, pick up a piece not resembling anything you had in mind and plop it right in where you have been working forever. Do you show your frustration or relief? This is the same feeling as being drawn in to do something. Do you try to make it fit? Or step back and regroup to try again? Once again the choice is yours and you have to have the judgement to decide whether it was the right path or just another attempt to pass a little further into the maze of life.

> *Don't compromise yourself. You are all you've got."* ~ Janis Joplin.

## Chapter Twenty one

# Tattoos

Now looking at the lead in word to this chapter, many will say what does tattoos have to do with the title of this book? As a young lad, new to the military, I felt the urge to get several tattoos. I often commented I looked like a walking coloring book. In today's society mine look like nothing compared too many others you see.

The other day, I noticed the one on my upper left arm had really changed over time. It is a double rose with two ladies faces one on each side. It is the roses that caught my eye. The once bright red roses are now natural or white roses with red highlights. Unique in it's own, but it symbolizes the changes we experience as we move through our lives.

My father had a single tattoo on his forearm; it was also of a sailor woman's head. This tattoo once stood out so big and clear making his forearms looking like Popeye's. As he got closer to his demise his tattoo shrunk to a mere dark mass on his arm, I marvelled at the change as time went on.

I believe we are inspired to have a tattoo by our previous influences the selection we make sometimes could be questioned. In the end there is a story that can be related that helps to symbolize the selection.

From butterflies to flowers, snakes to skulls whatever you can dream of you can now see on someone's skin. Sports events to love one's names.

Kids today openly talk of tattoos like they are a status symbol. They talk of getting everything under the sun etched on their bodies not thinking that these stay with you for the rest of your life. If I had to do it over again I would definitely have dropped a couple off. Mind you I got a couple will under the weather and as I recall it was my friends that were to get the tattoo and I was just along for company.

One time we were taking my buddy to get a tattoo as a parting gift after his bachelor party. He really wasn't with us on the last part of the event so we picked a naked girl in a champagne glass. The next morning when he woke up ready to fly home for his big day. Did he realize what had happened? He made a quick stop at the tattoo parlour to have a bikini added to his fair maiden. To add anything with the previous setting not healed intensified the pain he had to endure. But little did he know, once he arrived for his marriage ceremony the whole event was called off any way. We viewed it as if we saved his life in the first place, for his future bride to dump him that easy.

Many military personnel get military related tattoos some thanks to another guiding aren't visible by the naked eye. My one friend for example had a set of lips tattooed to his butt that said "Kissed by the Captain". Something better left hidden at the best of times. But with that story several more come to mind and I will leave them to the reader's imagination.

> "You may lose your most valuable property through misfortune in various ways. You may lose your house, your wife and other treasures. But of your moko, you cannot be deprived except by death. It will be your ornament and companion until your last day". ~Netana Whakaari of Waimana

## Chapter Twenty Two

# Images

My father was never one that would say he ever seen anything that symbolized something else. When he took sick, I helped renovate the bathroom to accommodate my aging parents. We took out the bathtub and installed a walk in tub which allowed my father to remain in his home longer. Once the tub was removed the flooring had to be replaced to accommodate the new layout.
With the type of cancer my father was dealing with, the urge to go to the bathroom was greater. As his disease intensified so did his medications. He would sit on the toilet and look at the floor; he noticed a face on the floor. When he was finished his business he called me in to show me this image. I seen it there was a face. Every member of the family had to go in the bathroom and view this image. As time went on we found several other images in this flooring pattern. We always told him they were his guardian angels.

I went back home on Mother's Day weekend. I went to the washroom and looked at the floor sure enough the same images are there it wasn't just our imagination taking us through a period of pain at that time.

I must admit though I to this day when I see a different patterned floor I do look to see if a warm face design is implanted in the design. Are these images a form of subliminal messaging meant to move us in a direction of spirituality? A message that we are being cared for in our times of need. That we only have to open our heart to feel the power of healing for the ones still travelling their destinies here on earth.

I think we all see images at one time or other. In a dismal room, a chanced image in the shadows or a fleeting silhouette moving close by. Our guardian angels re-assuring with their presence that salvation is near at hand if we seek it. To stimulate the seeds to action planted perfectly in our hearts. We all have heard of stories where people have been visited by a person just before their passing. It is amazing that these situations happen and we have the conscious awareness to know that this has happened. Are these types of images completing a preordained task they had to complete prior to departing from this earth?

Why can we lay out in an open field on a warm summer's day and watch fluffy clouds drift by symbolizing anything we can imagine through our own designing eye? It is this quality that adds beauty to our existence, a cloud, a song, a bird to identify just a few. We can see beauty in anything if we put our minds to it. Then where do so many go wrong? Are there hearts so closed that they cannot visualize beauty in anything? I think this is true for many, the things they conjure up in their minds over shadow any outside semblances of pure wonder.

On a recent flight, I looked out my window on the plane and marvelled at the mosaic patterns outlined on the earth below. Squares and rectangles of every shape and size with circles and ovals blended in. Splotches of forest dispersed here and there, what magnificent images were outlined below. Water traced its way in different areas leading to lakes, rivers and canals. I seen Niagara Falls from 36000 feet and if you didn't realize that there was a 350 foot drop you could never tell from that height it just looked like several rough white areas in a stream of water.

During the homecoming festivities in my hometown, I quickly realized that even though many have been living their lives away from the town they grew up in the desire to renew old memories touches everyone at some stage of their lives. We each carry the seed planted through memories and the desire to confirm the existence of something lost over time. A chance meeting, an old story or just an exchange of information there is a purpose why we get to have these people pass through our lives again.

## Oh My God It's Happening

*Oh my God it's happening,*
*A message straight to my heart.*
*A message oh so sweet,*
*Before my day did start.*
*An angel called to wake me,*
*To wake me from my dreams.*
*A voice so welcome, so divine, so sure*
*A voice oh so pure.*
*Oh my God it's happening,*
*My angel she brought me love,*
*She held me in her arms.*
*I reached up to touch her face,*
*I took her to our special place.*
*Deep within my heart.*
*Oh my God it's happening*
*An answer to all my prayers.*
*A special person to wow me, to cherish*
*To love me as her mate.*
*To walk our mile together, willing to greet our fate.*

*Author – me*

"The best portion of a good man's life - his little, nameless, unremembered acts of kindness and love." ~William Wordsworth

> "A visionary is one who can find his way by moonlight, and see the dawn before the rest of the world."
>
> -Oscar Wilde

### Chapter Twenty three

# The Truth

I am a firm believer that the truth will set us free. I have practised this thought most of my life. I have found every time a person stretches the truth their whole body language changes. Their gestures become more erratic and their eyes never really focus on you.

To hide from the truth has the same consequences; a person never truly deals with their problems. They skirt around the issues at hand, not wanting to be found out. It is really hard to hide from the truth. No matter what you do the truth has a way to find its way to the surface.

Something is happening; something big is going to happen. Just look at the big names that have fallen from grace. If that is happening at that level and visibility, just think what is happening at the everyday common level. We hid from our fears; these fears are compounded by miss truths.

The court of public opinion is passing judgment on the behaviours of their fellow man. Will there be a change such a dramatic change that our values revert back to the righteous? Is this change going to set off a chain of events that will lead man to his own demise? The changes that are coming will be momentous, whether biblical or from the acts of man, there will be changes. The messages we are receiving on a day to day basis are clear, they are open and they are evident something is changing in our world. These messages are forcing us to realize that we need the truth to survive. These messages aren't hidden they are clear cut and open, not subliminal in nature at all.

I know we all have to make changes, to face the truth in the process absolutely has to be a given. As it is written the meek shall inherit the earth I believe that time is fast approaching. A seed that was planted and has brought forth its fruit and mutated to accommodate the will of some. It is time to replant, the seed with the values it was meant to portray.

My second wife made a special point of highlighting how bad men were that played around on their spouses. How terrible, we men were and on and on. But when all was said and done who left who for what? Was it because all men are evil? Or was it that maybe all men should be evil? Or if I make them hurt so bad they will show there true colors and be evil. Any way you look at it, The Truth will come to the surface wait and see. Hopefully she can find a man that will live up to all her expectations. And really do it for her. Then the truth will be out in the open for sure.

At one of our children's birthday parties, we setup a video camera and left it running during the entire birthday. At one point we left the room and our young son proceeded to pull this girl's hair. This torment got completely out of hand. After the party we sat down and played back the video of the party and were appalled when we seen the hair pulling incident. We confronted him and even though the evidence was right before his eyes he lied about it.

*Eyes Closed, Too Hear*

What makes us take such rash steps? I recently heard of a similar one where my nephew had burnt his fingers on a car cigarette lighter and he claimed he had hot pizza at lunch which burnt his finger. It took more than a moment to finally confess he was wrong.

We definitely have to watch what we wish for. Truth will take over and what we strived for from deceit will come back to visit us. But it is the truth that will set us free. Not saying the outcome is what we wanted in the first place. I like to think I have learned something beneficial from everything that has happened in my life.

You will never be happy if you don't stop falling back, if you can't forgive and release your past. Things can only haunt you if you let them. The hurts of people are only remembered if you refuse to forget them. With an open heart a person can learn to move beyond this. You can either live or just exist. You can either be the hero or the victim.

The seed of truth must survive.

> *"A true friend never gets in your way unless you happen to be going down."*
> Arnold H. Glasow

> *"Speak your truth, even if your voice is shaking"*
> - Lissa Rankin

## Chapter Twenty four

# Auras

I recently had a very dear friend ask me if I have ever had any experience with auras. I said yes, matter of fact my aura is a shade of blue which signifies energy. She confided with me that her aura was white and she has been refused readings on two different occasions because it is so pronounced. To bring out your aura is very simple you merely have to have a light background behind the person and concentrate on a spot on their forehead for 30 to 60 seconds. Once you totally focus on the selected spot, a color will engulf the face and this is the aura.
Every aura has different meanings identified thru the color. White has a meaning of divine. There is a lot more to the explanation, I am merely expressing this fact in a simple form to make the point.

    An aura is another way we move into our spirituality that defines us as a person. Its influence is ever so present to our purpose on earth. I believe we are receiving subliminal messages from our past, we don't realize they are even there but we are totally aware of their presence. These subliminal messages are key to the seeds planted in our hearts. These seeds dictate the power of our aura.

*Eyes Closed, Too Hear*

Some people have the ability to see another's aura just by looking. The person's body reveals it's aura at all times, the shades of color can vary to some degree by the influences around it.

I think there are a lot of things we should be seeing and we aren't. For one reason or another. Why are some blessed with the ability to see auras or read palms or tell fortunes unless we have the potential ability to possess these powers in the first place? I have seen several fortune tellers in my life and I would honestly say I only met one that I wasn't impressed with. All the rest told me information I was already aware of usually adding in a few more details.

I have met people that are absolutely afraid to hear anything outside their realm of comfort. If these people were told they have a certain color auras they would be heading out the door in disbelief.

I view our life as a set of gears in order to make the big gear turn one cog; we little gears have to move through many cogs to get that end reaction. These many actions consist of such things as auras, horoscopes and mystic readings. Touched by everyday life, its trials and tribulations, influenced by love and pain. Then if we didn't gain enough, throw in a sickness or two and a couple doses of doubt. Mix it all together, fall back to the bottom to start over again and then see what color you might resonate. Yes we definitely have an aura, and I would love to think mine has a perfect blend to accept the best from my fellowman.

To inspire me to pass on my best image and offer a helping hand. To be recognized as that type of person would really be special and a seed worth planting for future generations to aspire to nurture.

Couple with auras one can find influences of their guardian angels. Everyone is guided and protected by their guardian angels I feel I am under the influence of several. The angel of writing, the angel of judgement, the angel of beliefs, the angel of music, the angel of astrology, the angel of my birth sign and finally the angel of the tree of life. These ones seem to have the greatest influence of where I am today and where I am heading for tomorrow. With the angel of the tree of life, the symbolization of the white dove has been present so much in my life. The bird of peace, I have often sought the meaning of why this symbol is so prevalent in my life.

> *"Words were never invented to fully explain the peaceful aura that surrounds us when we are in communion with minds of the same thoughts." - Eddie Myers*

### Chapter Twenty Five

# Our Choices

We have many choices that have a direct bearing on our lives. We can live and walk in fear. Afraid to take the steps we were destined to take. The fear that suppresses us as our own individuals. A fear that gives the control of our lives to someone else. Afraid of the tomorrows of our life, the future and beyond. A fear that never knows an end just repetition until the cycle is broken.

We have the choice to follow our spirituality to follow the guidelines established to manifest our inner being. The laws of life passed down from generations. The laws that today are being interrupted to fit our current lifestyles and faltering. If we hold the spirit in an open heart and build his temple there, we can only achieve the satisfaction we strive to maintain in this life. Turning our back in disbelief can only lead to our demise.

We have the choice to offer power. A power that is for the betterment of mankind. A power that is not meant to manipulate or control another person. An ability to lead without exerting absolute control to enforce our ideals. We all need a level of power, to exist, the ability to say "NO" or "STOP" that just isn't right.

We have the ability to know ourselves. To look within and mould our lives in a righteous manner. To know the direction we follow is ours and is meant to be. An ability that doesn't harbour hate or judgement of our fellow man.

We have the ability to love. This ability has to start with ourselves otherwise it can't be shared with others. If we don't love ourselves the other choices fall into jeopardy each one facing its own toll. There is such a fine line with love it is so easy to falter, turn our backs on it or even walk away. A choice that is often never afforded a second chance to experience true joy by the offending party. The victim of a failed love, if humbled will often be granted their inner desires. As I have stated before without an open heart, you cannot establish a strong foundation in a relationship. No matter how hard you try. Some people just can't grow plants they kill them every time, so it is in a relationship it dies no matter how great it starts off without love your seeds die. The grass on the other side of the fence turns brown just as easy if it isn't nurtured.

We make the choice to get married. We take the vows bestowed on us, and then something happens to so many and they stop. They let themselves go, no further input required, snagged my spouse. How many reasons or times have to be outlined? How much hurt has to be experienced before you realize that you had a part in this outcome? We live in a world of blended families, to the point in some circumstances it is hard to realize which children belong to which parents. To be a survivor of a single marriage is an accomplishment in itself and desires the highest praise as I see it. Our world is spinning out of control; the time is quickly coming where a correction will take place. A correction so astronomical that it will shake people to the very core. I have noted a very drastic change in many young people and change that is taking on a whole different life. I have noticed many young people are referring to a sense of religion that I haven't seen for quite some time. Maybe it has something to do with the latest slant in our everyday communications of 2012, the end of the Earth, Global Warming the list goes on. Whatever is fuelling this movement, it is getting more evident in the day to day dialogue expressed through our various social Medias. I believe the seed has been planted; the fruit it bears will have a direct bearing on the longevity of mankind on this earth.

We have the choice to create our lives in a manner that is meant to lead to fulfillment. Once again it can take on the image of a false fulfillment that is only as valid until the next controlling desire or a total fulfillment that completes us. What we create is what we create; it is under our control and only under our control. We must take the action to change it either way.

The choices we make are directly influenced by the guardian angels so ever present in our lives. So many of the guardian angels that influence me are silver angels or passive angels. The drive I received to write this book was inspired by the silver angel for writing. As stated in this book not everyone is inspired to write a book. To put your thoughts into words that are so profound that one's interpretation could be misconstrued merely by the reader alone. To feel you have a direction that must be put into written word for others to read at any given time, to read as a source of encouragement in a dark moment. Whatever the motive, I am truly influenced by a power other than mine.

Another choice that has been with me forever and this I have again, I have eluded to and I have known forever, the tunes I wish played at the end of my life. To have that sense of direction from a child again can only be influenced by none other than a guardian angel. The tunes themselves make the hair rise on the back of my neck. I have heard a good many songs in my life but these are the ones I come back to, too mark the end of my life. The celebration of life through the guardian angel of music.

> *"How wonderful it is that nobody need wait a single moment before starting to improve the world."* Anne Frank

> *"Each time a person stands up for an ideal, or acts to improve the lot of others, or strikes out against injustice, he sends forth a tiny ripple of hope, and crossing each other from a million different centers of energy and daring, these ripples built a current that can sweep down the mightiest walls of oppression and resistance." - Robert Kennedy*

> *"Success is not to be measured by the position someone has reached in life, but the obstacles he has overcome while trying to succeed".* Booker T. Washington

## Chapter Twenty six

# The Butler

I have always been one to extend my serves around the house. As I have previously pointed out I could cook a full course meal at seven years old. Laundry no problem. Company coming, what would you want me to serve? That was me. The family always joked that I was the butler. Anyway a couple years back, I had gone back to help my mother by doing a few renovations for her. This one day we went shopping and I seen this manikin of a butler it stood about six foot six with his white hat on. I thought about it and went back the next day and bought it. While I was at mom's the butler stood at the front window and caused quite a stir as people drove by.

When it was time to drive home I laid the seats down in my car and laid him there beside me. I put his head at the front end of the car. Mistake number 1. As I was driving down the highway here's these blue eyes staring up at me watching my every move. Now this trip is about a ten hour drive. The first hour was enough I stopped and got a green garbage bag and placed it over his head, perfect the eyes were gone.

Next distraction was his right hand was up in a OK position where the thumb and index finger touch. Mistake number two. As I am driving along this manikin starts rocking back and forth. Making it look like it is waving at everyone as we go by. A cop parked along side of the road sees this and he stops me. He asks If I needed something because he sees me wave. Then he spots the manikin with the bag over its head. You know where I am going with this. He asks me what was under the bag. I proceeded to tell, he nearly wet himself laughing so hard. I had to show him the eyes on this thing because they really looked real.

I thought the way he left me shaking his head I would be stopped by every cop on duty that day. I would imagine this will be one of his stories to tell for years to come to his descendants. From that day to date the butler has worn sunglasses.

Dad had a statement he would drop any time the situation was right. He would say "Next time around I going to be the woman, they get to do nothing". He did this on purpose just to get a rise out of the women around the house. And without doubt he had a taker every time that would respond in one way shape or form.

It is amazing how one thinks they are doing more than their fair share, while others do nothing. That's why I always like to say, walk a mile in my shoes, before you criticize. I have seen both sides of the coin and have felt the wrath. I guess once you pull your hand out of the bucket of water and you leave a hole, then you have room to talk otherwise just bite your tongue and walk away. To me it is a no win situation.

Reflecting on the path we have to tread; like the butler, one can tirelessly be convinced to serve knowing that no achievements are made without, commitment, hard work, and discipline. Not everyone can walk that path, but one of their own choosing.

> *"Blessed is the servant who loves his brother as much when he is sick and useless as when he is well and an be of service to him. And blessed is he who loves his brother as well when he is afar off as when he is by his side, and who would say nothing behind his back he might not, in love, say before his face."* -
> *St. Francis of Assisi*

## Chapter Twenty seven

# Procrastination

I was at my son's school not too long ago to listen to the speeches presented by the school body. One speech caught my attention given on the topic of procrastination. We all procrastinate to a certain degree. Our lives seem to always have something more important to do so we put off till tomorrow what should have been done today. No exception to the rule, we carry this into so much of our daily and spiritual lives. Not knowing if we even are afforded the right to have a tomorrow. If your spiritual house wasn't in order and inner peace had not been achieved would it be worthy to think you would make it to your rightful reward.

This is an area that so many procrastinate on. Many say when I get older I will worry about that. Just as many young die as old and in some age groups the young bypass the old. We procrastinate in our relationships; we think if we ignore problems in our lives such as a marriage, we will get beyond them. Wrong. If we don't correct the problems as they arise, they only manifest till there is nothing left to fix. It is a natural tendency to seek comfort.

To merely dream of an action is to procrastinate. It may start as a mere conversation very simple in nature and slowly evolves into a common bond. If we believe this bond corrects our situation and we don't do anything about the initial fault it will only repeat itself as at another level of procrastination.

There are people who procrastinate to procrastinate. They have absolutely no sense of direction, blundering through life, day by day, wishing that tomorrow will be better. Taking no action, what's so ever, afraid to see change? Our world is moving far too fast to live like that. A blink of an eye and another year is gone. A blink of an eye and a life is gone.

To live a life where the life you are living is to appease others, eventually turns to hate. We tend to over indulge, we find comforts in other areas, none that are healthy for either the body or the mind. There is always someone that will recognize the beauty you have to offer and help you beyond the fears of procrastination. If you find someone that feeds on your weaknesses for their own benefit, the same feelings will only manifest and carry on.

Then there are people who think they haven't the resources to take action. Each day they wish for changes but do it? I believe this form of procrastination only compounds itself far too quickly and a feeling of defeat and loneliness takes over. We are all guilty of a certain level of procrastination. Because as soon as we put of something for a period of time we are procrastinating. Once we take corrective action, we move ahead. The key is not to move from one to the next and leave important parts of our life by the wayside without realizing it.

How many times have we heard this statement "If only I took the time to….". We all procrastinate that there is another day to get things done. My middle sister wishes she did her grandmother's hair one more time. My other sister wishes she handled several things different. We often wish we would have taken the opportunity to say something to someone at one time or other. I wish I had started recording family stories sooner. Stories that have the potential to be lost forever.

My daily prayers have removed a large area of my procrastinations. I am achieving a direction that will resolve so many things I have put aside for another day. I also believe I had to achieve certain skills in order to make the changes and improvements in myself. Really through repetitious prayers it eventually brings the subconscious mind in line with the conscious mind. Once both facets of the mind are in line habits are easily formed and become a way of life. We can visualize are dreams and make them become a goal to work for.

## **Six steps to help you beat procrastination**

1: Simple be honest with yourself don't take refuge in the "It-will-only-take-a-minute" rationalization. People "keep going and going" on these only-a-minute jobs. "Turn it around. Realize that many jobs literally only take a minute, so let's do it right now. It's only going to take a minute."
2: Prime the pump. "Once we get started, we wonder 'Why did I put it off'?" Make a deal with yourself to work on a task for 15 minutes -- almost anything is endurable for that period -- and with resistance overcome, momentum to continue usually takes over.

3: Shut off your e-mail, msn and your phone. Make a deal that two hours later you can check them.
4: Individuals weak in emotional steadiness, conscientiousness or organization need to break down tasks into pieces, and finish one piece at a time.
5: Self talk. A person plagued with self-doubt -- not living up to other people's standards -- needs to say "This isn't the end of the world. This is just the way I react emotionally" instead of moving away from the task.
6: Use mind-ful meditation by focusing on your breath. A recent study confirms that this simple practice builds concentration power.

*People watching, Truth is, everybody is going to hurt you; you just gotta find the ones worth suffering for." -Bob Marley*

## Chapter Twenty eight

# Meditation

Meditation is a great way to relieve stressors. If you find you are dwelling on negative thoughts it is worth your while to spend that time eliminating these pain sensors from your life. A very easy technique that has quick results is to imagine the pain and rate it on a scale from zero to ten. Ten is the strongest or highest.

Now vision the body as a whole entity taking in every aspect of your inner being. Breathe into this body, filling the entire body exhaling slowly and deeply cleansing every cell. Do this several times. Smile from your heart to every cell in your body.

Ask your heart the question "What is the most important to me right now reveal it to me right now". Focus on the essence. Now think of the pain you had rated when you first started. Quite often the number will end up being less even after the first attempt. Repeating this technique will make it disappear. Your energy centres will quickly move to take you through this process with any stress related problem. They will redirect your energies to a positive nature.

This works very similar with love. For a person to experience spiritual sex, they have to start by getting in touch with their spiritual plane. Listen to their body, relax their mind, and step outside of the physical realm. To see a partner is to look past the body and into their spirit. To see their hopes, fears, dreams, and know what it is they need.

This has also been called the telepathic relationship, which is a connection with a partner that allows us to communicate by sensing mood, feelings, and sometimes even thoughts. A good exercise of its understanding is synchronized breathing. While embracing your partner, take each breath as they do. Feel their chest rise, the air fill their lungs, and the release of each exhalation.

As I pointed out in the previous chapter when we bring our conscious mind in line with our sub conscious mind only then can we achieve our dreams. Meditation is merely another way of expressing the same thoughts. To offer several ways of viewing the same principles can only enhance the simplicity of making positive changes to ourselves.

Many people have a mistaken idea that all thoughts can disappear through meditation and as we enter a state of blankness. We have certain times of great tranquility when concentration is strong and we have few thoughts. Then there are other times, we can be flooded with memories, flash thinking or even making plans. It's important not to get mad at yourself. Remember that you don't ask for your thoughts. Memories and feelings can come and go without our volition, yet we don't have to be controlled by them.

I find the more I get into the writing of this book. The deeper the thought process seems to take me. It has because a sense of meditation, to the point where I see words in my mind so vivid that they have a light auras around them. It depends on the chapter, if I come up with a thought that fits into a different chapter the visualization isn't as pronounced. These thoughts come to me at all times of the day or night. It is amazing where the mind takes its direction from but it is very evident the direction is real. As real as one's interpretation to a story to another. I have shared snapshots of this book to various people to feel the response coming back. To question how a certain chapter was viewed gives a different answer from each person. This is what I want to achieve, because we all think different, we react different and we have different stories that come into play when we relate to different life stories. It is like a message in a bottle, if you don't know where it came from and you don't know the circumstances can you be afforded the luxury of interpretation? I say yes. Our own.

Have you ever lain on a grassy knoll looking up at a blue sky watching the clouds slowly drifting by? Your mind goes blank, not a care in the world, a simple thought might enter and leave but you just lie there. You are in a state of meditation, now if you can force yourself back to a situation you would like to change and think of it as you lie there and let your mind work on just that one item. If you drift off for a moment your mind will come back refreshed and the problem you were thinking about will have less meaning.

> *"Love is what we feel when we realize we are one"* --- Timothy Freke

CHAPTER TWENTY NINE

# Christmas pudding

As a family growing up my mother made this Christmas pudding every year and topped it with a hard sauce. It would be steamed prior to serving and the aroma filled the house. Each person got a serving with a coin hidden inside. A coin for luck in the next year. This family tradition was one of few that we shared but right now it stands out as one that came from the heart. The bonding of a family in tradition has to be a gift heaven sent.

Like in this pudding the blending of ingredients to form a labour of love, not knowing if this year's pudding would match all or exceed expectations. The hot pudding would be dished out just prior to serving and the hard sauce cold from the fridge would slowly melt blending over the entire dish. As kids my sisters preferred the hard sauce to the pudding but the deal was they could have more if they ate the pudding. My mother used to make the hard sauce ahead of time and my youngest sister would always find it and sample it.

My brother in law when he first joined the family and had heard so much about hard sauce and he was so eager to try this. My sister pointed the hard sauce out on the table, he quickly took some and smashed it into his mashed potatoes. Boy, he says, this is really sweet! He was quickly told it was meant to go on the Christmas pudding.

### Mom's Christmas pudding
- 3 ½ cups Flour
- 2 cups Brown sugar
- ¼ tsp. Cinnamon
- ¼ tsp. Ginger
- 2 cups Suet
- 2 cups Currants
- 3 ea Eggs (beaten)
- 1 cup Water
- ½ tsp Baking soda
- ¼ tsp Cloves
- ¼ tsp. Nutmeg
- 1 tsp. Salt
- 2 cups Raisins
- 2 cups Mixed peel
- 1 cup Orange Juice

*Place in pans or heavy bowls. Tie cloth or foil securely over pans and boil gently 2-3 hours.*

### Hard sauce
- ½ cup soft butter
- 1 cup icing sugar
- Vanilla or rum extract

*Mix well and drop from a spoon onto a cookie sheet and let harden.*

> "The wise man does not expose himself needlessly to danger, since there are few things for which he cares sufficiently; but he

*is willing, in great crises, to give even his life
- knowing that under certain conditions it is
not worthwhile to live." - Aristotle*

## Chapter Thirty

# Dreams

Every family has their own dreams. And once related another memory grows. I have such vivid dreams and feelings I would love to express. I know there is a person out there that someday will share my heart. The dream where feelings are mutual. We all dream of winning a lottery at one time or other in our lives. But if we won would we be any happier?

I think not, I believe our problems would intensify, our moral values further challenged. The people that entered into our lives would always be in question after that. Like what are you really here for would be the first thought to mind. This not to be cruel, rather to highlight the greed of today's society. I would ensure that I would spread my good fortunes to the ones who truly deserved without being judgmental. The children would gain from this the most, but unfortunately not right away. It would be placed in trust for a time when they could really appreciate it.

My dreams are really more for health and happiness. We all have a need to be loved more than anything else in the world. A need to have our hearts opened to the wonders and joys that our placed before us. My true dream is to see everyone achieve that feeling in their lives. If I had any seed to plant and pass on it would be just that.

I recently watched a movie "What Dreams May Come" it held thoughts that moved me as if it were part of my life being told. There were things that happened that touched me. Mind you maybe it is the time of life I am in but many of the movies playing seem to be sending subliminal messages to me lately. I love to watch movies; I let them play in the background as I write. They stimulate my brain cells and cause more memories to reappear.

I recently had a very vivid dream that took me back to Adam and Eve. It brought me to modern days to a point where two modern day people were bought together through a spiritual intervention. These two people were a product of today's society duly separated in their own right from marriages that went wrong. Basically if there is no open love or companionship, these relationships were over and a new life was meant to begin. The direction as with the forbidden fruit was not to judge or direct to let the open heart have control. If they were meant to be together pure judgement would bring them through. I thought right then and there isn't this so reverent to put each one in control. There are no forced decisions. It is a spiritual attraction a prayer answered from the heavens above. Who gets to decide a sin is committed if it truly is guided through an open heart from a power even greater than one conceived from an outright infidelity or lust from adultery.

I just realized something very interesting, I am typing away the TV is playing in the background it is on the movie channel. I find commercials distract me. The movie playing is an oldie "Some Time Next Year" and it fits right in with this topic. This not the first time this has happened lately.

What are the connections? What is the meaning behind all this? It is not like I am watching the movie and then finding the motivation to right something. It is exactly the opposite. I write a thought move to the next and "BAM" something come on TV that relates to what I wrote earlier.

I was working on the chapter "Flowers" when this happened and I came back to insert this thought here.

## My Ode To You

*I long to hold you in my arms*
*And gaze into your eyes.*
*To stroll along our garden path*
*And share our inner vibes.*
*To close the gap between our hearts*
*And function just as one.*
*Remaining free as individuals*
*To mould our common fun.*
*I long to hold you in my arms*
*To tell you thoughts so near.*
*Knowing the life we share together*
*Can be lived without fear.*
*A life that can be so very special*
*Where open hearts do flourish*
*I love to hold you in my arms*
*And leave the bad behind.*
*To think of only joyous thoughts*
*Till the end of time.*

*Author – me*

## Visions

*My lifelong dream is growing*
*It is really taking shape.*
*I've always had this drawing*
*Too make it to this place.*
*I believe God's hand is guiding us*
*I feel his heavenly touch.*
*Taking me to my destined love*
*A love that means so much.*
*This feeling is so cosmic*
*This direction is so clear.*
*To have a prayer answered*
*Is music to my ears.*
*To follow in his love is our destiny*
*The path that is laid before us*
*Has a further meaning yet to see.*
*A meaning that once together*
*Under God's smile he will move us*
*To where we are meant to be*
*I feel his plan is working*
*It's growing in our hearts*
*Bringing us together to where we have to start.*

*Author – me*

*"Be brave enough to live life creatively. The creative place where no one else has ever been"* - Alan Alda

I awoke from a dream by a clap of thunder, yet I was still sleeping, it was a dream within a dream. I was told in order to find the purpose to life I had to go back to its simplest form. We need to live in love, with respect and cherish every living being. We can give thanks for every creation without a monetary contribution. We have to remove certain words from our day to day conversations such as hate, kill, murder and destroy. One must look at history and remember the worst people known to mankind had followers, yet so did the meekest. We will reach out for any sense of hope and follow blindly in trust to survive.

## Chapter Thirty one

# Humble

It is hard to be humble when you're perfect in every way. When that song came out it took our family like so many by storm after a few drinks for sure someone would start to sing it. I can honestly say I was probably one of the ringleaders.
Having lived through so many life experiences I found the path I was following was far from humble. I had to hit rock bottom this last time to realize that my life had to change. The values that I was raised with had moved off to the wayside and needed to be realigned. It wasn't that I was cruel or mean. Nor was it that I was unfaithful it was more like my heart had come to a standstill. I got to recognize my faults before they really became a problem. I believe that I had to re-adjust my life to fulfill my purpose in life. I was put here on this earth to carry out a specific function. My life experiences were my stepping stones to learning to be humble to move to the next phase.

Humility has moved deep into my life and I feel the rewards I am now seeing are the benefits of this realization. I know the path I have to follow is starting to lie out before me.

*Eyes Closed, Too Hear*

When I was little my mother had her tea leaves read and the woman reading them said I was bound to do a lot of travelling in my life. To date that has been very true. I know I am not finished, my destiny still has me on the move. Where ever my calling takes me I know humility has to form part of my next mission. Whether it is just another stepping stone or taking me to through to the end of my life. I like this new challenge because of the starts already forming in front of me. I look forward to this merging fate. I know it will be so rewarding because there is a clarity forming in my heart.

I had to become more humble to close my eyes to hear. The joyous voices talking to me stimulating the dormant seeds to germinate and move me further on. We have the ability to move through so many realizations within the silence of our own mind. The things we manifest there can have a drastic impact on the rest of our life. To move to a level of acceptance, to grow from the experience and round off our life. It is at these moment's we are at our weakest and satin's influence has the ability to corrupt even the purest thoughts. To be humbled to the point of being used is another thing, we allow ourselves to be reduced to mere puppets to justify our existence. We all deal with being humble in different ways. As long as we maintain our dignity at the point of final realization, it is a lesson well learned.

> *"Believe in yourself! Have faith in your abilities! Without a humble but reasonable confidence in your own powers you cannot be successful or happy"*
>
> *Norman Vincent Peale*

*In the end, we will remember...the silence of our friends" --- Dr. Martin L. King*

## Banana Bread

3 smashed bananas

½ cup margarine

1 2/3 cup sugar

2 ¼ cups Flour

½ tsp Salt

1 ½ tsp Baking powder

1 tsp baking soda

½ tsp vanilla

½ cup black coffee

2 eggs

Beat together eggs, margarine, sugar and black coffee. Add dry ingredients and beat until creamy. Add bananas and blend. 1/3 cup of finely chopped nuts or fruit can be added if desired. Grease and flour bread pan. Bake at 350 F for 1 hour.

## Chapter Thirty two

# Comfort foods

It seems every time we have problems, the first reaction is turn to comfort foods. Our body knows it needs something so it is a natural reaction is top up our spent resources. Our body craves either salt or sugar and sometimes both. The more a person slips into their dilemma the more we tend to eat. Once it becomes a habit this extra eating is hard to stop.
Like with comfort foods if we don't nourish a craving heart. We feed it with all the wrong vices. The heart moves to a lost place where it blunders along. We reach out to our safety spots and where there are so many changes. We tend to look for simple solutions. It is at this point if we don't start to work out our problems we have to take corrective action. If we start to work on ourselves and love what we have. We start to mend. We have to learn to love ourselves before any other love can truly exist.

Once we reach this point the sun starts to shine again, we start to mend and our heart opens to love again. The choices we make are choices that have value. They are choices that will survive. We are offered better options that we can live beyond because they are heavenly founded. Inspired by the seeds planted by our heavenly maker.

A pure heart has great values it is not judgemental, it knows how to forgive. A pure heart helps others without malice and monetary rewards.

My life has been blessed with the knowledge of people fitting both sides of the coin. The cruel and greedy really have no life. Their problems seem to control their very being. And they voice them as if someone else is responsible. We all know these people. They are not hard to find, we just need to stop to hear them. On the other hand, the gifted are rarely seen or heard they seek no rewards. They appear as guardian angels, good Samaritans suddenly before us to guide us along. Their names we rarely remember once our problem ceases to exist.

A bowl of popcorn, snuggling in to watch a movie is comfort food to me. The people we get to share this with are loved ones we have feelings for. Even though our destinies may vary we achieve comfort from the heart long before the new seed is planted.

Now if you asked my youngest son what his favourite comfort food would be. Without a doubt he would respond a good ole brownie covered in a thick chocolate icing.

## Chocolate Brownies

- *4 tbspn. Cocoa*
- *2 Eggs*
- *½ tsp. Vanilla*
- *½ tsp. Baking powder*
- *½ cup walnuts (optional)*
- *½ cup margarine*

- 1 cup Brown sugar
- ½ cup Flour
- Pinch of salt

*Blend cocoa in melted margarine. Beat eggs, add sugar and beat until fluffy. Add vanilla, flour, baking powder, salt and nuts. Pour into a 8 inch pan . Bake at 350 degrees for 20 minutes. Let cool*

## Icing

- 1 cup icing sugar
- 2 tbspn. Cocoa
- 2 tbspn margarine , melted
- ½ tsp vanilla
- 5 tsp cream

## Chapter Thirty three

# Lotteries

I thing every member of the family buy lottery tickets at least once a week. It is more of a past time to me I say I am buying wallpaper one square at a time. Very costly wallpaper and really not a neat design. The odds of getting hit by a truck are greater than winning the lottery. Games of chance. Why do we go there? Now if we take it one step further we also do this in our lives. We take chances that are in hopes of bettering ourselves, without making drastic changes.

So here we are again, back to the point I have been making throughout my book. In order to facilitate a positive win we have to look into our heart and love what we see. To gain the rewards we desire and have our prayers answered. We need to start inside ourselves. Simple, then why do we keep gambling on something different? Most the time we aren't willing to view the consequences; we would rather struggle with pain than take the first step to move beyond our inner hell here on earth.

Life is really a lottery, but instead of playing it and gambling. We are living it and gambling. Gambling that every move we make is going to take us closer to our ultimate jackpot. Our ultimate jackpot has nothing to do with money. The older I get the more I realize that money has an importance to survive but that is it, everything else has to come from something different. You can have all the money in the world, but be confined to a life within four walls never to admire the beauty around you. Or confined to the wall of your mind and not seeing anything period.

You take a look at the drug abusers or addicts; they took a gamble, played the lottery of life and lost to be caught in a period of time or a vice that will never allow them to see their true potential. The ones I feel sorry for are the ones that got trapped in addiction by someone else's hand. In some cases a onetime mistake that carries on for the rest of their natural lives.

This also holds true for sexually transmitted diseases. An act of Lust that just keeps passing on and on. This type of sharing person really has a lot to answer for and the gamble they have taken should never go overlooked.

Our society is another form of roller coaster we have our highs and lows, twists and turns. Sometimes it is viewed that we are standing on our heads. Extremely liberal at times then so very conservative moving to the will of public opinion. Our lottery of life. One would like to think that eventually a common balance will be achieved but unfortunately greed rears its ugly head and the process continues on.

Sometimes when you look at these different communes are they far off from the perfect society. If they all live in unity and have no superior ruler and work to the betterment of all equally who am I to judge. They may have the winning ticket but to what magnitude would it work?

Once we move through the open heart and begin to blossom, every person we meet gives us greater insight into life. It is amazing. The exchange could be just a smile but that is positive signal rather than a freaking scull. Every warming feeling moves through the heart as new found energy we change our walk, posture actually our view on everything.

There was a recent thunderstorm that my three younger sisters lived through. There city was revenged with this storm. The damage was extensive all around them, severe flooding and property damage. They went out and surveyed the damage and felt very fortunate when they got home. Their damages were so minute in comparison to others like winning a lottery they felt very fortunate.

A lottery doesn't have to be monetary to feel like you won. It can also be the luck of the draw. The person ahead of you driving down the road has the accident or the light turns red and you stop to miss something falling off a truck. I had one of these experiences when I was younger. I was following a truck when a piece of lumber flew off the back of the truck bounced off the road in front of me and came straight for my windshield. That split second and so much passes through the mind. It hit the top of my windshield on the metal trim and flipped off. I won the lottery that day, no questions asked. If it was my time I hate to think where it would have passed. Let's put it this way there would have been no generations to follow, I was that young.

Another time, this time I was a teen; driving down the road in a 51 Ford pale green in color; something snapped in the steering as we approached an "S" curve in the road. We left the road the car rolled on to the passenger side, I slid over on to my buddy's lap again the world flashed by in mere seconds. I reached out and grabbed the steering wheel as we hit the shoulder of the "S" curve the car bounced back on its wheels. I slid back into the driver's seat and regained control. We managed to take that car back to the cabin passing the toll booth on the way in merely missing it by inches. Spinning the steering wheel freely until it caught to re-align the front wheels to move to the next correction. A person would only try to do something like that young today the brain would kick in and we would call a tow truck. As soon as we stopped, my buddy stepped out of the car and barfed. I was so shaken up it didn't hit me till much later. My father was not impressed to say the least. Good old cars though, very little damage other than a piece of trim scrapped off the passenger side. Today half the car would be gone but we would have seat belts to put on.

Have I won a lottery? Yes, several times, and walked away to talk about them. Can I plant a seed? Yes. We are not invincible, especially when we are young, when the gap in our brain hasn't filled in. We all take chances that are what makes us human but remember like the lottery not everyone wins.

> *"We're so busy watching out for what's just ahead of us that we don't take time to enjoy where we are." Calvin & Hobbes*

## Chapter Thirty four

# Poems

Dad's second oldest sister was my godmother she was an aspiring poet. She got recognition for several of her poems. She was a very deep thinker and expressed herself as such. She took an interest in family history and she had a collage of family pictures that I would give my eye teeth to have my hands on to add to my tree. I never really knew her that well even though her influence is ever present.

Now take this one step further; why was she destined to be my godmother? Was she to hold the seeds that needed nurturing in my later life? On the outside one wouldn't even notice, except the footsteps that I have followed add essence to what I am doing now.

I believe we all hold the quality to express in rhythm but the mood has to first strike us. Whether that mood is through love or merely an object. The desire to express ourselves in rhythm has to be stimulated. It is like putting words to music and looking at some of today's songs how can you go wrong with one or two words.

I often have a feeling I was a "scop" or a wandering minstrel in another life moving from hamlet to village spreading words of prose. Singing life's stories of real cosmic events. I feel these seeds are ever present and have meaning to me.

Put me in a party situation, that trait wants me to keep the party rolling. Where does this come from? Was it a planted seed from the past? I believe this so, my dad's father performed a level of entertainment all his life. He had to get that from somewhere. The information I require takes me back to old England why not imagine that a minstrel was involved. Better than a horse thief or an axe murder to plant their seed of hate. I would rather be an influence by happiness, any day. By nature, I am happier when I am offering of myself rather than receiving, a gift that so many haven't the ability to do. Like a minstrel, all I can offer is me, everything else is artificial. Phony, a fake to myself, a liar, call it what you want, these are all the negative attributes that can influence the same sphere. I know deep down inside all these influences are not for me, my minstrel nature swings me back to a loving poetic me.

Whatever seed has been planted in my past experiences, I long to express my ability to still love what is left around me with a forgiving open heart. A heart that carries a rhythm, a tune, the seed to future joy.

My youngest son tagged himself as the jester on his profile for a good part of a year, if you stop and look at the irony of the whole situation could this come back to fall in line with my thoughts of the wandering minstrel? Who knows? The fact is there and he wasn't influenced to use this name by me. It was something that he was influenced to use. He comes by his traits honestly; his uncle, his mother's brother has taken on a life in entertainment and has done numerous shows. It is always said the fruit doesn't fall too far from the tree. If it runs in the family, the seed has been planted. My son loves to dress in unique and outlandish outfits just to see the response. It is a trait that one, would love to see where it will actually take him in his life.

I think anyone can write a poem. The key is to have a basic thought and then if we take our time a person should be able to construct something. I think the key is not to get obsessed over making everything rhythm. Everyone writes poetry and songs about a love lost...what about the dreams that never come true?

Here's one that has made me smile, to think this probably happens all the time. Someone has taken the liberty to express their thoughts on flowers they know nothing about. But this is the point I am trying to make. We can write a poem, a collage of words on anything.

*Eyes Closed, Too Hear*

## *Thanks For Remembering Us*
## *Dana Gioia*

*The flowers sent here by mistake,
signed with a name that no one knew,
are turning bad. What shall we do?
Our neighbour says they're not for her,
and no one has a birthday near.
We should thank someone for the blunder.
Is one of us having an affair?
At first we laugh, and then we wonder.*

*The iris was the first to die,
enshrouded in its sickly-sweet
and lingering perfume. The roses
fell one petal at a time,
and now the ferns are turning dry.
The room smells like a funeral,
but there they sit, too much at home,
accusing us of some small crime,
like love forgotten, and we can't
throw out a gift we've never owned.*

### Chapter Thirty five

# Quotes

Another aspect of life that intrigues me is a good quote. It is like a snapshot in time that meets all occasions. Some quotes are very moving, deep and meet the very need. Some quotes just add quips that move us into maybe a mere laugh. They inspire a smile and add quality to our life.

We all use a quote to aid in our expression. My father had quotes for almost anything out of the clear blue if the conversation was dulling he would merely say "And into the valley of death rode", the conversation would inevitably change. Another as I pointed out in a previous chapter, "Next time around I'm going to be the mother".

One I find I use quite often is "A pound of sugar goes further than a pound of salt". I f you go into a situation bitter and looking for a fight that is exactly what you end up with. But if you go in nice and sweet you can get your point on the table open to further discussion more often than not. The odds of the situation turning sour have been highly defused. A better situation all round. Another similar one is "Butter wouldn't melt in their mouth" in other words they were so calm and cool that things just come off very smooth.

*Eyes Closed, Too Hear*

I recently ran into a person that was so within them self, every point was I, I, ME, ME. So in my reply I simply stated "A person so wrapped up in them self is a very small package" point taken by many that had noticed this person's actions but still missed by the offender. In writing this book using "I" so loosely has been a problem for me right from the very beginning. I keep going back and try using a different phrase to say the same thing but to no avail and go back to the original. For this I say please forgive me it is only a means to express a point. I am not trying to negate the other persons involved but rather not to speak their thoughts either. My goal is to inspire a thought that will motivate the reader to replace my examples with ones of their own in which they can relate.

From there I can say my seed has been planted and everyone can relate with phrases that have inspired their lives. A great quote can make such a dramatic difference in how a person expresses their thoughts because it removes the "I" from the equation. It adds a level of knowledge so profound from another mouth. It may have been the only profound thing they ever said but with today's technology it is readily spread to the world instantly.

> *"When people ask me, 'What can I do?'--I say, 'Two things. One, you must realize that, unlikely though it seems, your little life does make a difference, what you do each day.' And secondly, leading from that, people must think a bit more about the consequences of the choices we make each day." --Jane Goodal*

*"Real charity doesn't care if it's tax-deductible or not."* ~Dan Bennett

## Chapter Thirty Six

# Politically Correct

I was on town council for four years. I was correct 50% of the time and wrong the rest no matter what topic. You can only please at best half of the people. I would like to think I am very liberal at heart. I believe in helping the common man so needless to say I strived to remove the extra fingers dipping in the public purse. I think with anything if you want it you pay for it. Period. User pays bottom-line. That way you can spread your resources to the maximum with full benefits.

Having said that I believe a person should be able to say almost anything as long as it is not offensive to someone else. If we care for every person with an open heart we have achieved true meaning. Why should we have to watch every word, every phrase, every movement and action to ensure we are politically correct. A person that is under that much scrutiny is not the one with the problem to hide.

If there is a skeleton in the closet it will rear its ugly head to bite your behind every time. Just push the right buttons, politically correct or not out it comes.

I held similar positions in the military taking an active role on our mess executive. From president to entertainment chairman I loved to work with people. Their thoughts and actions always influenced the success of every endeavour taken. When people are treated as you would like to be treated they will move mountains to make it happen.

I have seen it time and time again if you go out of your way to help the underdog the benefits come back tenfold. People that abuse others eventually get their just reward also. Not saying it is what they expect. I believe the worst punishment would be to live till you were 100 plus with no friends or family left to care for you. Alone with your thoughts and no resources to escape.

It doesn't matter what we do in life, if we present ourselves in the public eye we are subject to being politically correct. Whatever we say is open to scrutiny, there is always someone willing to step up to the plate, quick to judge and point out the error of your ways. A prime example is today's media; they have you getting up in the morning till your lights go out at night. What a life, if that is what you want your fifteen minutes of fame. No thanks, I might pick my nose or scratch my butt or anything else that might be news worthy. You just don't know what someone else will assume is politically correct to act on.

Being politically correct is just another form of mind games. I absolutely detest mind games if you don't do this that won't happen. You are being held captive at the will of others. I find if you play into mind games they just compound themselves so quickly. Some people thrive on this style of control. If you don't do this by the time I count to ten this is going to happen. No it isn't you are going to make this happen so you can control the situation. Period. Call it how you want it is a mind game to make you feel politically correct. Control your own mind and open your heart and then we have something to talk about. Look for the goodness in everything and you will see it, eyes closed too hear.

Communication is very important, but a lot of the times, people forget that there has to be understanding and giving. You have to give, in order to receive. If you don't give, and just take, you're selfish. If a person is selfish, no matter how amazing the partner is, it's a dead end.

Don't try to control the relationship. Two people are in it together, and there are no captains or leaders. Two equal people. If you give out ultimatums and boundaries, you're controlling. You have to be able to let go of yourself and control because it's abusive if you don't compromise. No matter how politically correct you feel you are stop and think what you are doing to the other person. Know it, believe it. Period.

> *"A hero is born among a hundred, a wise man is found among a thousand, but an accomplished one might not be found even among a hundred thousand men."*
> 
> *Plato*

#### Chapter Thirty seven

# Flowers

Flowers their natural beauty, we all have our favourites; they have their own stories. We either grow them or buy them, as the need moves us. We express our love through flowers and we mark our dead also. In off season, we even buy either silk or plastic merely because they are such a part of our life.
I have known people that could kill a plastic flower or at least bleach it beyond recognition. I believe we give off a vibe that these living vessels feel, when they are complained to and neglected them, they to wither and die. If we treat them with happiness and nourishment like in our open heart they flourish and grow to pass on their beauty in seed.

My father so liked the poppy we had one engraved on his headstone. The poppy held him in comradeship with all his military friends. It reminded him of his long lost brother who died before this in a country only meant to visit at a more peaceful time. His brother is buried there with the friends he died with since 1944. He died a hero in his own right he went back to help an entangled soldier entangled in a barbed wire obstacle and died through his attempt. His only remembrance was a stained glass window in a local church and then the government named a northern lake after him after the war.

I am partial to a rose. I have several tattooed on my body for some strange reason the red color has disappeared and they now resemble white roses. I would like to think there is a purpose why this red color has disappeared. Red roses say "I Love You". White roses with red edges signify "Unity" and pure white alone have several meanings "You're Heavenly", "I'm worthy of you" or innocence and purity. Each one in this respect suits me just fine.

I have always been a bit partial to the hollyhock; they stand so proud against a fenced backdrop, great background filler with such an array of vibrant colors. They come back faithfully every year and last well into the fall. What more can a man ask for, not labour intensive and low maintenance. They don't bite you as you walk by.

Several years ago the residents of our beach; at the lake where the family cabin is; decided to plant some flowers at the entrance to the beach, the local union took offense to this and felt their jobs were in jeopardy. So they removed these plants. The story hit the local press and shortly thereafter it had gone national. My mother was interviewed and had her fifteen minutes of fame. The article was titled "Where have all the flowers gone" and it was submitted by my one sister. I recently went home and someone had taken the liberty to remove all the excess flowers from the headstones at our local cemetery, this was Mother's Day weekend. The fallout was about the same as the article done years before. I submitted my statement to the editor of the local paper with the same title. A repeat in history which only a handful connected to the previous article.

The seed was planted again and flowers are now viewed as a common site on the local headstones. Flowers are as natural to grieving as they are to expressing love; it is the thoughts that pass through a person's mind as they make a decision that will haunt them for the rest of their lives. What must they feel like after they stop to think about their initial action? I personally don't even want to go there.

It is bad enough going to a nursery to buy set out plants and they die a couple days after because the dirt they were started in gave no foundation for them to exist in until they took hold. Mind you when you pay good money to get plants to early, put them out and the frost kills them you wonder what has changed. We have the same amount of frost over the same period of time every year. There are some things in life you don't get to rush and beautiful flower beds are one of them. If you manage to get them beyond the frost stage and the rest of the landscape hasn't progressed fast enough the wildlife will eat them because they are the only green things around.

Don't get me wrong I love gardening it is a great source of relaxation if done properly. But can also be a nightmare if no forethought and planning to go with it. Like humans some plants just don't get along with others, the nature of the beast. Some like to go out in the wilderness and introduce local wild flowers to their flower beds. Knapweed is one that kills everything else in its path.

We try to put flowers everywhere in our lives, this year is a funny year where we have had more rain than normal, and mosquitoes are a problem. So a lot of time has been spent looking for ways to defeat these little blood-sucking pests. I recently found an article that stated catnip eats mosquitoes so immediately had to pass it on. I then thought; with a slight glint in my eye; it would be funny to see fields of these plants around trying to get rid of our dreaded insect. But if it works who am I to question, let's get planting. More seeds, from the past everything we need to survive is here on earth. Know it, believe it.

## Chapter Thirty eight

# The Dance

One thing our whole family likes to do is dance. We seem to get started at quite a young age and it carries right through our lives.

My parents' life together started by going to a dance. As the story goes my mother was to go to this dance in the next town with this one person and he cancelled out. She went any way, she caught the train to the next town. My dad looking for something to do was told to go to the dance also. They meet and went to the dance together and danced all night. The return train was one hour after the dance was finished. The station was locked so they sat on this long wooden box. It turned out to be a rough box so dad retold the story over and over there they were a stiff below and one on top.

My mother and I like to dance the polka, but on more than one occasion I have left her sitting on the dance floor. I seem to have energy plus when it comes to a polka and it takes a strong person to keep up with me. This is where I will stop tooting my own horn.

The dance I have a great problem with is the butterfly; I always seem to lose one partner along the way. I remember going to one dance as a teenager. My buddy and I were selected to do the butterfly with this older heavy set woman she literally threw us all over the dance floor, into the sideline chairs and watching spectators. That was an experience I don't care to do anytime soon.

One Halloween celebration I dressed up letting my feminine side take a stroll on the wild side I did rather well all evening a good many didn't realize who I was. I stayed away from the dances that would be a telltale indicator who I was fun. Then the "Bird Dance" came on and I forgot myself for that split second and started right into my down and dirty routine and sang along with the words. The gig was up my identity known. One dance changed the whole evening. That was the last time I let my feminine side out for a stroll, mind you I have also had some semblance of facial hair since then also.

Both my parents and my oldest sister and her husband have been known to go to a dance be the first one up and the last one to stop. Many a time, a remark would be heard how great the evening was because there was someone on the dance floor at all times. It is amazing how simple the action can leave such lasting memories.

I definitely get into the swing of the music, adding my own personal touch, not saying it is good bad or indifferent to the ones that know me they just say "OH that's him". We have lived through such a time where so many things have changed and dancing is one of them. The fears remain the same as you watch from the sidelines at a child's first dance how they stand off on the sidelines longing to get up enough nerve to ask some cutie for their first dance ever. Or you go to a wedding and you get to sharpen your first skills at dancing with a relative. Who through their experience you learn to make the moves that allow the nerve to be expressed with a stranger or a secret love. Life's challenges, all expressed through a series of body movements labelled as dancing.

Yet when sitting at a function it is remarkable how many sit along the sidelines and look longingly at the dance floor. They think they can never get up again that this action is only meant for the young at heart. It is amazing how many stuffed shirts get offended just at the types of music played. A view that could so easily be changed through an open heart. Another seed planted a challenge to be carried on into future generations. Live it, Love it and Do it because time slips away on us so quickly.

The good thing I am getting older and have mellowed somewhat. We have been taught right from a very young age to try to dance with anyone that asks. I have had a good many partners in that respect and found some a real challenge and they probably say the same about me. I do like to over emphasize some gestures that take a little time to get used too. I believe there are some that are never really accepted. To be that restricted that you are embarrassed to be on the dance floor makes me laugh. I have seen some pretty weird stuff and have lived with it. Boils right down to self expression I guess and the fear to show it belongs to the one that owns it.

## Chapter Thirty nine

# Carpentry

Our family have all been self taught carpenters. My dad and I have both helped many of the family carry out renovations throughout our years. One instance always stands out my mind.

My middle sister's first husband called on us to help put an extra room in the basement of their new house. The brother-in-law a budding carpenter was tasked to put a plate to hold a light switch in the studding. It was in his nature to take shortcuts so instead of walking around to the newly studded room. He decided to reach through to hammer a nail. This move created a blind spot. You hear this "Smoosh" and the longest inhalation of air. His hammer drops. And the loudest " Geeeeeeze" emanated from his mouth. Then he started to dance. Dad and I turned to catch the action and started to laugh. That ended his rough-in carpentry experience and he quickly became the advisor on this project never picking up his hammer again. This story has long survived their marriage.

Sometimes such a simple renovation makes such a lasting impression. I have seen this so many times, one ninety year old house I owned was just that. Every wall was an outside wall, even thought they were on the inside of the house. This house started as a one room home and as the family grew so did the house, a room here and a room there. A different roof, a roughed in attic. Then I bought it, the wiring was prehistoric and no insulation so the job slowly took shape as we lived in the house. Take one room at a time, crack it open change the wiring and insulate as required. Quite a process but very rewarding in the long run. This wasn't the only old house I did so I knew what to expect as I started to crack it open. The treasures you find in the walls and under the floors can be quite amazing.

I found a newspaper grocery ad dated back on my dad's birthday away back to 1937 where for example a one pound can of floor wax was 23 cents, and to dry clean a 3 piece suit was 65 cents. What a time this must have been, the end of the dirty thirties and pre second world war. Just imagine the stories that could evolve from this simple newspaper ad. This newspaper was placed under flooring that at the time was probably the state of art and thought to last forever. If I never chose to redo that floor I would never have found it. It could have been buried in yet another layer of flooring for another couple generations. I was meant to find it because of the relationship to the date and my father.

This other old house I redid we put a grey slate floor in the living room. It turned out fantastic and added definite characteristic to the style of house. We had the opportunity to return several years later, there was this floor stacked outside the back door. We asked to look inside to see what had changed since we were there. The inside was totally gutted once again a quick lesson in reality of one man's palace is not always another's kingdom.

Another house I redid we added a sunroom off of the kitchen, where we installed a hot tub which made quite an addition and was ideal for relaxing after a hard day's work. When we moved from that place we took the hot tub with us and the new owners filled that space with aquarium tanks to me a real waste. But who am I to say that was right or wrong.

Basically the changes one makes in their day to day lives are not permanent and must be treated that way. Things as in carpentry change at any given merely by the one holding the tools and the vision at the time. Each time we take on the challenge to change our home or location we introduce a bit of our influence into the mix.

The key as in any construction has to be the firm foundation we decide to build on. Without that no matter what we do it will not stand the test of time. And with the speed at which places are constructed now a day's one really has to question, where these places will a couple generations from now. The labour of love once introduced into a masterpiece is now replaced by a schedule, a deadline and a profit margin rather than one's castle and his family home.

## Chapter Forty

# Words Ending in "tion"

Revelations by mere definition explains itself. The act of revealing.

Dad as he was lying in bed nearing the end of his life had a couple times where he had his own revelations. One instance my second sister's two daughters came to see their grandfather for what could be the last time. One niece promptly steps up to the edge of the bed and says in a high voice "Hi Grandpa". He looks up and says " You don't have to holler I am not deaf but could you step back your standing on my pee-tube it is pulling on my (I will use a politically correct term here) connection". My niece jumps back and says I can't go back in there again. The next morning dad has this moment he needs to see all the family. So I go out and gather everyone up to listen to what he had to say. He looks around and counts noses and says " Who's missing?" I go back to the living room and tell my niece grandpa is asking for you and he knows you are not there. She went back in to see him.

Humiliation. I mentioned dad's pee-tube he was a very private person in that respect and he was mortified to be hooked to this plastic bag. He was so scared of becoming detached from this apparatus that he asked that no family dogs be allowed in his room. He feared they would pull it off.

Another time while he was sick my oldest sister comes into the room where I was talking to a cousin. She says "I think we have a problem" I walk down the hall and sure enough there's dad sprawled back in his chair. His false teeth were hanging out of his mouth and by all appearances he looked like he wasn't breathing. I walk over and pop his teeth back in his mouth, he jumps with a start. Stepping back said calmly "You have company". We never told him what had transpired that day. Even though he would have had a good laugh.

Frustration. As in any large family there are always leaves of frustration and ours is no different than any. My niece recently moved to another province so she went down to change her driver's license. She has had to jump through hoops trying to make this happen and has been reduced to a nothing because of bureaucracy at its finest. It has been three months now and her dilemma still persists and no driver's license.

Determination. So as with the previous example she is determined to see corrective action taken. I had a similar situation happen to me. I had bought a new fridge and stove back when Coppertone was the in color. The fridge kept acting up so I would call the repairman. He would look at it and say there is nothing wrong but I will change the control just in case. This went on several times and tempers were rising, I told him he was spending more time in my home than I did and asked if he wanted me to setup a cot for him. Still this fridge acted up, so I wrote a letter to the head company and said I was going to paint it lemon color and put it on a flatbed and send it back to them. Finally a rep from head office comes in he puts a 24 hour monitoring system on it and they identify a defective compressor. If I had given up on this, it would have remained a problem as long as we owned it.

Condemnation, the act of condemning. We are all guilty of doing this at one time or another in our lives. It is very easy to condemn one person's actions without knowing the whole background story as in anything there is normally two sides to every story and we should be aware of both sides before we assume we know the complete situation. Then I go back to my other statement what makes you a judge? I have had a considerable amount of time to mull this statement over in my mind and I wish I had this knowledge earlier in life. So now knowing this I can say another seed planted and hope someone else will learn from this experience.

Consideration or deliberation, the act of considering, careful thought. So many of us are so wrapped up in our own things we fail to consider the thoughts of others around us. We say whatever comes to mind, not thinking for a minute that it may also mean something altogether different to a person listening to it. We have all been in a situation where cursing and swearing are common place, but as in anything it is not always accepted in the same light by everyone exposed to it. I have seen little children barely out of diapers that could make a trooper blush by the language that comes out of their mouths. You know good and well this child is in a heap of hurt from day one of their impending school years.

Damnation, the act of being damned. My mother's father was the walking example of this it didn't matter what was going down, you were damned if you did it against the will of the Lord. Heavy statement and as I pointed out in another chapter an interpretation that followed him right through his final days of life, he had to pay for his judgement and damnation that he extended on his fellow man, to me it wasn't his right to extend that belief on to anyone else. If I say I will be damned it is one thing but you will be damned for your actions are not for me to decide. Your day of reckoning is yours and yours alone that's where the judgement will truly take place.

Isolation, how many people can you think of through their own thoughts have isolated themselves from the pleasures of true life. They have robbed themselves of the given right because of their inferior complexes that if dealt with and or recognized would have offered a completely different outcome to their life. What happens when they get to the pearly gates and asked what did you accomplish in your life? Oh I was too scared of myself to see the rest of the world. Well go back again and this time do it with an open heart and appreciate everything presented before you. Do I have too? Yes!!

Admiration, a double edge sword. It can be viewed under two different lights. In this case we can only admire ourselves rather than all the beauty supplied by the people around us.

Not to be outdone by administration, where one runs everyone's lives around them and can't administer their own. They feel if they control everyone around them people won't notice their deficiencies. Control is good to a certain extent until it gets overbearing then it is no more fun. Another seed planted for those that need reassurance.

Interpretation a real biggie. Every situation we touch has to be interpreted in our own minds. It depends on everything from mood, right down to the person involved. The thought process can come from a gut feeling to a similar event from our past. It turned out this way last time so I will over compensate on my input this time to alter the results in my favour. But does it? If we feel we have made poor judgement quite often we have and if we don't take corrective action. The interpretations only compound themselves.

> *"Ability is what you're capable of doing. Motivation determines what you do. Attitude determines how well you do it."*
> *~Lou Holtz quote*

## Chapter Forty One

# The Cabin

A good many years of our family life were spent at the family cabin. There could be a book written on this topic itself. Dad built this cabin himself. In the beginning he vowed it would never have electricity, a phone or indoor plumbing. I would honestly say due to the ambience of this setting several generations were actually conceived here.

Quickly becoming friends with the neighbours, it was decided to build a fireplace down the property line so both families could share at anytime. A good many parties took place around this area and once the fireplace started to crumble it was replaced by a fire pit. Generations of stories were told here sometimes nearing on true confessions. There were lots of laughs and memories.

Rolling back a bit, dad quit the bake shop and went north to find work. We moved to the lake for the summer, no electricity, no plumbing; no telephone, just mom and a hand full of kids. That summer was remarkable to say the least, how mom survived is beyond belief. Mind you shortly thereafter we had electricity and a couple years later we had a telephone. We were the only cabin on that corner of the beach that did have a telephone for a good many years.

The kitchen table was where all the kids would gather after an evening of fishing to watch as grandpa cleaned the catch and each kid got to poke at the guts and roll a real fish eye. Those were good times that have carried through the generations. Once the fish were cleaned and put away, the mess cleaned up, the table was a meeting spot for a game of cards or happy conversation.

May long weekend, the cabin is officially opened for the season. Everyone gathers to clean up the winter's telltale wear and tear. Projects are established for the year's upkeep. Water is re-connected, rain barrels set up, deck chairs are put out and flower pots are made ready. Over the next few weeks the cabin springs back to life for another season. After thanksgiving weekend in the fall the procedure is reversed once again.

At one time lights were strung every season and every bulb was tested. Now with solar and LED even that procedure is simplified good thing I guess because we all are old. Over the years we have seen many changes from our parents' initial dream. The cabin was built; to offer their children a summer they could afford at the time. This simple action planted a seed very evident for generations to come in our lifetime.

This cabin has seen weddings, family from afar, happy times and sad times; it's been a meeting place more than the home in town. The cabin in where all these conveniences were never meant to exist. These in them self gave our dad extended time at the place he so loved in the last part of his life.

As a child I ran around our beach at every chance. I would go from one end to the other exploring every area looking for something different to do. We could find almost anything back then and try to haul it home. Bee hives, bird nests, unique sticks, rocks with different marks, baby birds and frogs. Those were such adventuresome days. It was so peaceful to listen to the trees swaying musically rocking you

*Eyes Closed, Too Hear*

too sleep. Then at the crack of dawn awake to the ranting of a flock of crows. The cabin offers all these things.

I had a chance walk through the cabin about a month ago to see how it survived the winter. There by the back door were dad's old rubber boots sitting waiting for someone to walk a mile in his boots. To carry on the dream that he left behind for his family. These rubber boots had survived so many events. They were there for a purpose then and they still are now for anyone needing to run quickly outside for something as simple as a few sticks of firewood. The tops are a bit tattered but they symbolize the relaxed atmosphere around the cabin.

Dad used a statement quite often "Up the creek without a paddle" and this has brought back to mind a story. My mother's parents came for a visit. Grandma had stated she would love to go for a ride in the canoe if someone would take her. Dad said he would love to take both of them. Grandma got all dressed up in her nice white pant suit and off they went. It was a very successful event, a lovely ride around the lake. They returned to the lagoon to park the canoe and dad say's to my grandfather when we get to the shore step out and hold the canoe stable. Grandfather did this but he took it one step further, he picked up the nose end of the canoe to pull it up further. Down it went, dad with the paddle in both hands to stable things, up to his neck in water. Grandma still sitting in the centre of the canoe and she was absolutely drenched also. The words that were said were probably heard at the cabin a few blocks away. The story has remained, even though all three are gone now by the seed that they planted.

One thing that happened as dad's sickness took hold was he couldn't find a comfortable chair or couch to sit on. Mom would find these deals on armchairs and couch sets and of course they would also have to pass the comfort test. Out would go the old and sometimes in would come one older as long as it met the comfort standards for the moment. One old couch has taken to the dump and it ended on top of refuse pile off to one side. On this one occasion, a few of the younger kids wanted to go see what the bears were up to. So off to the dump they went, to find a bear sitting on this old couch looking over his domain. It caused quite a laugh because every time a different chair or couch was brought in for dad's comfort we thought of the story of "The Three Bears".

Keys have always been a concern with a large extended family at the cabin. Mom has always had a fistful of keys which she was scared to throw out because she thought they belonged to the cabin. Last fall it became necessary to replace the outside door, so we took the liberty to change the lockset. The intension was to start fresh with all new keys and have any existing locks keyed to match this one. Wrong, the new key got mixed in with the original bunch and the same problem presented itself for the new season. It is amazing how something so small and shiny can cause such a great problem. It is time to stop procrastinating and resolve the problem before we are too old to remember what the problem was in the first place.

There is one memory that sticks in my mind, mom used to take us kids to the beach everyday during the summer. She would pack up a lunch and off we would go. We would spend the day there and then she would get us back to the cabin in time to make supper for 5:30. This one day they had put a fresh coat of tar down on the road and she knew she still had to get home. She made her way down the road and the bottom of her feet had this hard pack layer of tar on them. Needless to say this layer didn't come off easy it lasted till at least Christmas. This became the standing joke

*Eyes Closed, Too Hear*

around the beach; everyone asked her if she had her new soles added to her feet for the summer.

When my father passed away, the family received a multitude of letters from friends that remarked that one of their greatest memories was the family tradition of making homemade ice cream at the cabin. The smashing of ice and hand cranking the cream mixture until it was perfect. The biggest thing was to be the one selected to lick the paddles clean. This seed was planted but also touched many outside the family

## Chapter Forty two

# Bears

This chapter could have very easily been combined with the previous chapter but after due thought I believe it can be a stand alone. I remember my first experience with bears at the lake. We used to use my dad's sister's cabin when we first started to go to the lake. Dad, a family friend and his son plus I went fishing this one evening. We had a fantastic catch and returned to the dock just after dark. We had to walk this dark path up to the cabin, lugging all our gear. Dad and his friend carried this big string of fish between them. There was this growl in the dark behind them, the fishing gear went flying, the fish were dropped and we all took off at a dead run. The bear enjoyed his late night snack that night and we had no fish left to clean.

    When dad was building the cabin, he often caught this big brute of a bear sitting there watching him. He would hoot and holler and chase it away. The bear selected his time to get even. Once the cabin was finished, and as stated we had no power. In one dark corner outside the cabin there was a hole dug to keep food cool. We called it our frog hole because frogs would crawl in there to keep cool. We used to haul enough food from time to cover a weekend. Well anyway, the frog hole was our fridge, one

*Eyes Closed, Too Hear*

night there was a great ruckus outside and the bear had finished the next day's breakfast, dinner and supper.

The bears would wander up on our deck, and as I got older I would run out with a canoe paddle and whack their butts to scare them away. One time after my youngest sister was born, my mother liked to have her babies sleep outside during the day in a pram, to get fresh air. Needless to say you can see where this is going, I caught a bear looking in the carriage and I was off scaring the bear up a tree. That time I went and got the forest ranger and had it removed because this one was too brave with a small baby around.

Over the years, bears have made their presence known but the smaller kids always get a kick in going to the garbage dump to see them in action. The cars all line up to watch this daily event. As I had mentioned in the previous chapter you can never tell what you might see even a bear sitting on an old couch, thrown away. One person's garbage in this case was another animal's treasure. We hauled some stuff out to the dump earlier this year and that same old couch a little rougher for wear sat off to one side. Maybe the custodians of the dump felt the same as we did and had witnessed how this bear liked to sit and oversee everything on it.

## Chapter Forty Three

# Travels

In the early seventies I sailed the fiords in Norway. That to me was one of the prettiest sights in the world. I marvelled at this beauty in nature and would love to make that trip one more time in my life. From there we went to Brest France and down to Portugal.

In Portugal I witnessed the cruellest treatment to man that I have ever seen. There was civil unrest when we got there and many riots were taken place. I saw people holding others on the ground and their fellow protestors jumping off cars onto these incapacitated people on the ground cruelty supreme. How could people treat their fellow man in such a manner? This was my first taste of such hostility and I certainly hope it is my last. I have witnessed since then similar situations on TV but they don't seem near as bad as in person.

We next sailed to the Azores and finally home, that was the furthest south I went with the military. All my other experiences were in the Canadian north. I have travelled all the dew line sites several times. Spent some time in Greenland and over to England but never further south.

Since leaving the military I have been to Hawaii and Mexico several times. I swam with the sharks. I have been to Jamaica. Travelled North America extensively and still seek another destiny I know I have to do. What drives a person to travel? Is it to find new things? Have seeds been planted in our past to travel like some explorer? Our family tree indicates we have had a lot of people who have done just that.

My grandfather took my mother and her brother to Nova Scotia this one year. My mother had been writing my father while he was serving in the navy and they had made plans to meet. The train arrived in Halifax; my dad wasn't there to meet them. My grandfather being a little impatient said he wasn't waiting around, so made my mother promise she would stay put until their return. Meanwhile dad shows up and being of the same nature said they couldn't hang around waiting because they only had a short period of time together. So off to Dartmouth they went. My grandfather and uncle return, mom is gone. My grandfather goes into a complete panic and begins to imagine everything under the sun that could go wrong. Mom and dad return a few minutes before the departure time of the train. My grandfather was so happy to see them return, he never got mad or made a scene over the events of their day.

I would like to take you along a different path of travels for a bit. When my dad was in his final weeks we were quite concerned over his movements. Not that it mattered what he did but rather we didn't want to see him fall in his frail weakened condition. We had mentioned this to the palliative care nurse that he liked to just walk into a room to see what was going on and they kept saying there was no way he had the strength to do that. One day we were all standing around talking in the kitchen and the palliative care nurse was there also. She asked if she could stay just a little longer and maybe have a cup of coffee because just the way our dad was breathing coupled with a few other signs that the end was very near. We were all talking very quietly and paying no real attention to the doorway into the kitchen when in walks dad and he says "What's going on here?" Well the palliative care nurse looked at all of us and could only say "We told you!" Her quick response was you are going to have to write a book about this someday.

Dad in his morphine state thought he had superpowers and we never discouraged his attempts to be with the family because he so loved to hear our stories right up to the end. When we offer support to dying parents and friends one tends to deepen the understanding of the blessings and burdens associated with their ability to enjoy their final time. We had to travel this distance together paying due diligence to the roller coaster of grief mounting in each of us. This final trip had to encompass his life, his dignity, his respect, his joy and ultimately his final peace. All the things I would like to think when my time comes are afforded to me. Another seed planted. We don't know who is next to walk their final mile, in my mind I would like to think I have left it easier to address for the ones' left behind. It won't be; every emotion has to be dealt with to heal. Each person has to take this step in their own stride. They get to travel the narrow path on their roller coaster of grief.

We all get on my mother's case when she uses the statement "Well next year when I'm not here" or "I will try to dance one more dance just in case I never get to dance again". Statements we are not ready to hear but we are all getting to the age where our check out time has no sidewalk guarantees either. Mom basically doesn't want to outlast any of her children. We have the luxury of being able to joke about it but it boils down to the one basic fact. This is her vice, her dilemma; longevity travels on her side of the family tree. As long as you have some semblance of health and get to your eighties you can go a long quite well.

*Eyes Closed, Too Hear*

On the return flight from a trip to Massachusetts, I had to pass through security at Logan Airport. They are using the new walk through x-ray machines and with this all pockets have to be empty, belt removed, the works. Anyway it was my turn to walk up to the machine, I step in place hands on top of my head and my shorts drop to my ankles. All I heard was OH MY GOD, thankfully my gotch had a good waistband. I just stood there until they said I could walk away, bent down and pulled up my pants and left. Shortly thereafter an airport police officer came up to me and asked my name, I thought does this have something to do with my already embarrassing moment, but alas I wasn't the person he was looking for. This reminded me of a flight I was on while in the military. We were flying in a Hercules transport aircraft and at the back there is a toilet off to one side it is covered with a cloth curtain so that you aren't open to the rest of the cargo area. Anyway this young officer had to go to the bathroom, the aircraft hit a little turbulence and he fell out of the "Johnnie on the spot" with his drawers down by his ankles. Funny at the time but now I can relate.

During my most recent trip to the Maritimes, I took my son down roads I hadn't travelled for thirty five years to say the least. As we drove down roads I hadn't thought of for numerous years a flood of memories flashed back to me. We passed an underpass where a good friend's life ended after a high speed run back to the nearby military base in a self induced state of intoxication. I related a story, where I had an accident after commenting on a girl in a bikini to a co-worker going to work a good many years before. I took him by a piece of land I owned, where I had such dreams of building a home in the country and here after all these years it is completely populated. The difference time makes, when you can relate it to the past.

CHAPTER FORTY FOUR

# Negativity

*There is little difference in people, but that little difference makes a big difference. The little difference is attitude. The big difference is whether it is positive or **negative**."* W. Clement Stone

I have had to deal with negative people all my life in one way shape or form. Is a cup half full or half empty it is a play in semantics? When you are dealing with it in a military situation it could mean a fine line between life and death. A negative person distracts the entire team.

On one occasion I had to deal with a pilot that made my entire crew do everything in their power to avoid him. The worse he got the worse they got. Finally one evening I took him off to the side. I had a little talk with him and made a couple positive points that he grabbed on to. Life definitely got better for you all concerned.

My career had me ear-marked for a position where I was to have a definite input into the careers of my fellow tradesmen. The powers to be felt I had a unique quality in dealing with people and an ability to defuse a negative situation. This has somewhat followed me through my life.

My first wife, once she was diagnosed with breast cancer we headed on a five year journey through the realm of negativity. One might say well you didn't have the disease. Right but I lived it. When my father went through his walk with cancer he lived it on the opposite sphere and his demise never really had a bearing. He wanted to see his sixtieth wedding anniversary, another Christmas and he would add something each day until he got too tired to go further. Even if his day meant to hear one more family story it was good.

My first wife extended such pain and self pity coupled with very irrational thoughts. A person was constantly walking on eggshells waiting for the next dilemma to drop. The bad definitely outweighed the good. The sacrifices made to appease her wishes, I would give my eye teeth to go back and change. They have become scars, that mark my life and crosses that I have had to bear. I feel I have accomplished my level of forgiveness from these situations.

One example I would like to share is she wanted so much to see both of her sons married before she died. I setup a garden paradise in our backyard so that our youngest son could be married there without added stress on her. Wrong, it was a fricken nightmare. Everything that could go wrong went wrong. It was a marriage that now when you look back was brought together for all the wrong reasons. It was a son trying to achieve his mother's dying wishes. They weren't ready, her parents didn't want anything to do with it and we lived every moment of that wrath because of it.

It was a time in our families' lives where if anything else could go wrong did. Starting with a spattering of deaths, a wedding, a funeral, a family striving to be non in-laws, wow we had a soap-opera in the offering. Bottom-line my son's first wife was afforded the opportunity to be with my first wife at the point of her death. This to me was her way of saying it ends here and shortly thereafter it did. I would like to think it was her way of planting a seed to correct, the mistakes she made in the latter part of her life. This seed bore fruit very quickly and changes were made to change the paths for the ones left behind. The negativity felt from this experience left a sour taste in many a mouth for a definite period of time. From this all I can say is forgive me, because I was the instrument played to make it all happen.

> *"Holding on to anger is like grasping a hot coal with the intent of throwing it at someone else; you are the one who gets burned."* - Buddha

> *"Choosing to be positive and having a grateful attitude is going to determine how you're going to live your life."* - Joel Osteen

## Chapter Forty five

# Argument

We all know people that will argue just to see someone else's reaction. It doesn't matter if it is black or white they will take the opposite point of view. My youngest son has that quality. He has spent more time out of school because of a stand he has taken. I can't fault him for it because he won't be a pushover in life. He just has to learn which battles truly need to be fought over. I believe that will eventually come. He would do well on a debating team.

I know some people once they start losing an argument will start throwing things and slamming doors. These people to me have a problem; they are good candidates for anger management.

If I find a situation needs a strong point of view I will investigate every possible fact and then make my stand. I would like to think the stand I take can be viewed in everyone's best interests. If there is a known policy, the end result is simple you follow the policy until such times that it can be changed.

I will use one of my favourite examples. I like to refer to a marriage of two people as the merging of thoughts, likenesses, dreams and hardships into one union. Simple, wrong it is a recipe for almost anything if one person tries to be the more dominant factor. Period. Live it, believe it. If the powers to be are willing you can argue over the dust on the TV to a Kleenex on the bathroom floor. You can argue over absolutely anything. My mother did it this way or your brother should have done that different. Whatever the situation, if the desire to have an argument is there, and both players are willing the game is on. Sometimes very productive but unfortunately if always one-sided becomes a thorn in one's side.

The first thing a person has to ask them self is this a by-product of my upbringing. Do I need to change? If the answer is "yes", then do it, don't carry your past into your new life. The next thing a person must ask them self am I trying to make a point? If the answer is "yes" make sure the other player understands the point and does it really have to start as an argument?

All thoughts do not have to be the source of argument matter. Stop and think about it. If you are merging two different cultures, two different lifestyles, two different ways of dealing with things there is bound to be friction. It takes time, patience and understanding to make this merge happen. Every influence can become "the problem". Plain and simple, treat the other person how you would like to be treated. If you need a spark in your life, don't make it an argument. The results in the end just aren't worth it.

Words can cut just as deep and take just as long to heal and as a physical blow to the body. Express your words from an open heart and listen to the answers the mileage gained could take you a lot further in the long run. "A pound of sugar goes farther than a pound of salt".

> *"Parents should conduct their arguments in quiet, respectful tones, but in a foreign language. You'd be surprised what an inducement that is to the education of children"* ~ Judith S. Marin

## Chapter Forty Six

# Humour

We all carry within our self the ability to be humorous. Some more dry than others but that is what makes us unique. I love to tease just as much as I joke around, usually going just a shade too far after all is said and done. My dad's side of the family were always more inclined to play a practical joke, we have had some real good laughs over the years. Maybe it also has something to do with coming from a larger family.

    A wedding is always the right atmosphere to inflict a certain level of humour by the virtue of having two nervous people looking to impress another family. I have played jokes on my nephew and cousins equally. I have gotten to everyone of my brothers-in-law at one time or other. Having said all that there are a couple different examples that come to mind. Stories go right back to my dad's father having sampled several concoctions prior to his daughter's wedding and losing them down her back just when it was time to take her memorable photos. A wedding meant to be picture perfect has been relived and laughed at for generations later. My aunt is the only one that remains and all she can say is "Oh Yeah that was a day".

    One thing with the advent of modern communications, we can share our humour at a moment's notice with anyone anywhere. It is fantastic; I wouldn't change it for the world.

When I first was going through the transition from married life to a life of a single older person, my sister and mother were sending me jokes, cartoons and anything uplifting to keep my spirits up. In days gone by that technology wasn't there, the support groups that were needed were never seen until for many too late.

I can find humour in anything, it could be the most devastating thing for some people but really if a lesson can be learned and it doesn't hurt someone else you may as well look at the humour in it. I will relate to a recent example that was a costly lesson for me but hopefully a seed planted for others. I went on this trip out of the country and like so many I have electronic devises for everything, one being an internet connection stick. I put this stick into the ubs port of my laptop and proceeded like nothing different was happening in my life. Prior to my departure I had asked my sister who worked for my communications provider to see if there were any changes I needed to do to curb costs. She did this check into my status at the same time I was away and she phones me in a complete panic. She says your internet air time is right off the map. I removed the internet stick from my laptop and phoned my provider the next morning. They assured me of my mistake, my costly mistake but the way I look at it if I hadn't found this out. I would have probably had to pay a considerable amount more because my youngest son and I are going on a similar trip very shortly. Matter of fact before my next bill was due to come in and we would have for sure been playing off two notebooks.

On the same token, we can view something like a person getting hit in the private parts and laugh. A person falling off something and we laugh. It is a knee jerk reaction we see something, our mind interprets it one way and then we realize we should actually be concerned to look at it in another way.

Sitting around the fire pit at the cabin with a cool beverage the stories would flow it was like being next to a confessional sometimes. Other times the humour was endless. The stories would always start off simple and they would build with intensity. One night my brother in law had taken out his spotlight to look for something after he was finished he laid the hot light on the seat. For some miracle unknown to this day he didn't quite burn the truck to the ground but he sure did a fair bit of damage to the seat. This brother in law is quite a bear hunter; he can go out and analyze what the bear has eaten. They then go to the area and hunt for the bear. Just by analyzing their scat, this one day he had left the camp and was gone quite a period of time so the rest went looking for him. There in the middle of the road, was a pile of scat but it wasn't bear, it was human. They finally caught up with him and mentioned they noticed the human scat down the road, he goes "Oh yeah, I had to go real bad, so I went." Then he was asked "What did you wipe your butt with?" He responded without hesitation "A Kleenex but I didn't leave it there because I didn't want anyone to think it was a human".

As long as in our level of humour we don't hurt anyone in the process, it has to be acceptable. If we find humour at another person's expense then it is a whole different thing. We have all done it at one time or another; it is an easy situation to slip into. It starts as a simple joke but if it is taken too far it becomes a form of bullying. The easiest thing to do is place yourself in the recipient's shoes once it moves from humour to upset. Then corrective action has to happen immediately. The humour of Borat, when the movies first came to air, is a prime example. A good many tried to copy that level of humour with sorted results. It was a means to agitate others. There are other shows that run on the same level of humour and can be taken the same way. The point to remember is these are all shows and to perform expecting the same results can really try a friendship.

I had a memory come to mind on a recent road trip. A good many years ago, probably in my first year of married life, my neighbours at the time had told us of this great place to buy chickens. The only problem was we had to clean them ourselves. No problem, my neighbour and I went off to buy these chickens, we got them home. Cleaned them all up, the smell was out of this world but we got it done.

I had cut some into pieces and we froze everything. My mother's parents were coming to visit for the first time, so we thought chicken pieces were a perfect meal to prepare. They were grilled to perfection, golden brown and culinary delight. That is where this description stopped, we sat down to supper and each with our own chicken tried to cut into them, nothing happened. They were like rubber, my grandparents tried to be so polite and managed to cut off little pieces to chew. We could have cooked these things with a rock and had more luck eating the rock first. Needless to say, dinner plans quickly turned to take out. This was a good laugh that stayed with us for a good many years thereafter. We learned very quickly that these chickens were ok if they were boiled for a period of time first then roasted.

Not too long ago we were celebrating my nephew's eighteenth birthday. It was a very pleasant evening, so we sat around the fire pit sharing different stories. One lead to another and he says the first word he learned to read and write was "Rubbermaid". "Rubbermaid" was the response. Yes "Rubbermaid". Ok share! He said when he was little he would ride on the tractor for thirteen hours a day with his step father and they would read the word "Rubbermaid" off the water bottle. First learning the letters and then the spelling. We all remember certain things that mark our lives and until shared does it really take on a special meaning.

Here is another good lesson where things can look perfect on the outside but very hard to palate on the inside. A seed planted and can be related to almost any life experience.

*"Maybe this world is another planet's Hell."*
*- Aldous Huxley (1894-1963)*

*You can observe a lot by just watching.*
*- Yogi Berra*

## Chapter Forty seven

# Joy

We can find joy in absolutely anything, from a birth of a child to seeing a grandparent admiring the results of their life. If we get to enjoy all our pleasures in life through an open heart the meaning has to be further compounded it is not clouded by doubt and resentments. Every time we help someone from the heart with no want of reward, the joy of giving is so wonderful and the results are far more bountiful. It all rolls back to the thought that counts.

Having witnessed my father watching something as simple as a parade going by with little kids waving back and the tears literally rolling down his cheeks to being at a function and the joy of being there for one last time written all over his face. To the knowing fair well, that the odds of seeing him doing this one more time, were quickly disappearing.

I think back of the joy of siblings getting together knowing this could be there last time together. My mother's father, his brother and sisters all relating back to times that you could hardly believe were parts of their lives. They would argue in love that their version of the story was the way it was but really it is all how we interpret things in our own minds. Slowly each one took their turn to leave this world but amazingly enough the joy they imparted on us remains. And so the seed is planted.

Joy in our family is ice cream. None of us can go by an ice cream parlour without having to sample one of the many flavours available. Big or small we are all the same. I remember my mother accepted a challenge that this one ice cream parlour presented as their way of working with their customers. If you were able to eat this giant ice cream monstrosity the whole thing was on the house. When you look at it a challenge not everyone would even entertain. The choices are really endless when it comes to ice cream.

It seems the greatest things we enjoy in life are also a vice. One of the few things that aren't a vice is anything that takes us back to family and nature. Joy like humour can come from any source. The slightest thing can spark a sense of joy. It is one of life's greatest rewards for situation that make us standout above the other living things on this earth. We can be at the bottom of the heap or at death's door and the simplest event will make us smile. A touch of warmth that passes through us and gives us those spark of pleasure.

*"I'm glad I did it, partly because it was worth it, but mostly because I shall never have to do it again"* – Mark Twain

> *"To love at all is to be vulnerable. Love anything, and your heart will certainly be wrung and possibly broken. If you want to make sure of keeping it intact, you must give your heart to no one, not even to an animal. Wrap it carefully round with hobbies and little luxuries; avoid all entanglements; lock it up safe in the casket or coffin of your selfishness. But in that casket- safe, dark, motionless, airless--it will change. It will not be broken; it will become unbreakable, impenetrable, irredeemable."* - C.S. Lewis

## Chapter Forty eight

# The Daunted

So many live their lives disheartened with everything around them. Is it their problem or the intimidation controlled by others? Either way the cycle in itself is not healthy and requires some sort of intervention or corrective action. At times we can be our own worst enemies; we have the potential to fabricate something in our minds until it becomes a reality. When the daunted feeling is induced by the intimidation of others, once realized must be corrected, the situation alone makes a concubine in your own right. This existing in a loveless state, held for no other reason than superiority over another individual to cover up their own inadequacies. A person has to be honest to them self over the "why", the why they are even there. If any answer comes back for the love of them self, then it could be acceptable with reservations. But nine chances out of ten the justification will be for the sake of someone else. Life is too short to make these sacrifices unless you wanted to be a righteous person dedicated to a higher power and nothing else. In this situation you still wouldn't be living under intimidation induced by the daunted.

I know several that have fallen under this category in my life and to a certain degree maybe I, myself can relate. Allowing your life to be humbled by other's actions and you have no input has shed a new light on my purpose. I have made up my mind to shed myself of this stigma and stand proudly on my beliefs. To do it my way with an open heart and the fellowship for people that really cares.

## The Daunted

*What makes us so daunted?*
*To live in fear in our minds.*
*To propagate uncontrollable spores,*
*Where sunlight can never find.*
*What makes us so daunted?*
*To walk our walk and not let out,*
*Our garbage filled in doubt.*
*When is it time to make the change?*
*To be undaunted isn't strange,*
*With non prejudiced influences it starts,*
*Found deep within one's heart.*

When we feel daunted who gets to open Pandora's Box? To release the evils onto our earth, according to ancient Greek mythology, Pandora was the first woman, created on Zeus' orders as a punishment for mankind. Her "box" (actually a sort of jar) contained many evil things, such as toil, illness and despair, but it also contained Hope. When the jar was opened, these evils as well as Hope were released into the world.

I know the feelings associated with this, to have the power to open the box and let all the evils of the world spew forth. To either clear the air or to turn guile upon the masses. To be moved in such a way ends up as the choice of the offender or offended. I clearly have seen what can fall out of Pandora's Box and I don't like what I have seen. To have the presence of mind and to be moved to forgive and open my heart has far better consequences and the guile can be left to someone else's demise and not mine.

> *"Most of our suffering is born from our lack of understanding and insight that there is no separate self. The other person is you, you are the other person. If you get in touch with that truth, anger will vanish"* --- Thich Nhat Hanh

## Chapter Forty Nine

# Rational

We are not rational at many times in our lives. We make changes that come from our inner thoughts and many times the amount of time expended to get there is not quite enough. Having said that many things happen in our lives that carry no realization of any rational thought process, we are merely the by-product of someone else's actions. Do we have to comply? No!! But many of us do, and that is where the problem manifests itself. We have bought into this thought process rational or irrational time will bear this out.

If you are a person that has to be right all the time, then you are not rational, period. Face it, Grasp it, Live it you are not rational. You are merely adding pain to everyone around you, because they are trying to conform to unnatural wishes.

If you are a person full of hate or negativity where nothing is good in your life again you are not being rational. There are a lot of good things happening around you but your mind is to closed to recognize them. Face it, Grasp it, Live it you are not rational. You are just exposing people to your garbage thoughts and they will soon turn away from you.

Not everything is bad, full of doom and gloom. These are merely tests to put us on a different path in our life. We are here for a purpose. Period. A purpose that is simple, it is directed by a pure and rational heart. Close your heart add allow any word ending in "tion" to play a key factor in our lives, we stop being rational. We make silly mistakes, to error is human. Once we have made these mistakes and allow them to persist in our lives then we can no longer say we are being rational.

To be rational doesn't mean you have to trade away your own inner beliefs. It just means you have to consider others around you and if nothing else use a few simple words like "Thank You". What you add with that is up to the individual. Just showing a little thought shows you can be rational when dealing with the people around you.

> *"We human beings are in search of meaning, in search of our selves...We are born for meaning...pleasure that is steeped in meaning. We are born as well for suffering... that leads to...joy: the struggle with ourselves and our illusions...to overcome ourselves"* Dr. Needleman

## Chapter Fifty

# Parables

Parables are a short narrative making a moral or religious point by comparison with natural or homely things. When done right there are no social or spiritual borders. This book in itself is a start to a parable. It brings past into the present on to the future by planting seeds of hope and love for generations to come.

Positive and simplified conversion of our thought processes through an open heart is a parable on countless levels. A person can say this smacks of religion, it may but by the mere interpretation of one's mind. To lay out a parable or story that everyone can relate to you have to add some logic. There are many that can argue a different point of view. This is fabulous, that makes us human, but once this enters the thought process the seed is planted. This seed will re-appear at one point in your life. You might only say I remember I read something on this subject at one time. Then my message in this book will have value and the seed has successfully been passed on.

Every person has a story. A story with many roots, it comes back as a parable when it is compared to another time.

Have you ever opened a person's dresser drawer after they have passed or their personal treasure chest and found keepsakes you never knew they had? The feeling is so eerie you have stepped into their parable their link to life. You could find a past, a present and only a hint of a future. A favourite photo, a poem, a ticket stub, a ribbon absolutely anything that contains a story and a memory. It is a link to a life from days gone by.

Say you open a book and it has a dried flower between the pages, you don't know where it came from, you don't know the story but you do know the feeling you feel in your heart at that first glance. A parable with an unknown story left to the imagination of the person observing it. If we allow our minds to develop a story, where would it take us? This is how innocent the discovery can be but the end result is also the creation of our minds.

I related to a story of the headstone I seen "Here lies a true friend" this one has really taken me. I would love to know the story behind this stone; it wouldn't be a pet sitting off alone in a cemetery. So it has to be human related, to me a form of a parable there is a meaning, a story, a memory.

Genealogy to me is another parable stories within stories each locked in time. So covet the pages of a family bible the diary of days gone by. Little notes, hand written records, touched by family at another time, their struggles, their dreams, their losses. Anything that can be thought of can be seen. Why would something like this be saved where so much is lost? Is it another example of a seed passed for someone else to grasp on to? I view myself as very fortunate to be able to say I have found so much where others falter. Is this my living parable? Or just another example of a seed planted for one such as me to share. To pass to yet another generation.

Modern day parables are a fantastic way to relate to others about your faith. We have all heard biblical expressions from the bible but do we really pay any attention to them? This book in itself is basically a series of parables that I have been raised to follow a good part of my life. The chapters in this book have all come to me at one time or another connected to a parable. Such a simple statement, but does it really have merit? I would say yes. Could I refer to a biblical statement to each? Again I would be able to say "YES!!"

Amazing as it is we can listen to TV commentator relating a whole story about any topic of your choosing and believe it. Place a biblical connotation to it and the theory is questioned. Yet when the facts are said and done. The predictions of the bible are not too far off the mark. What does it really take for some to stop and pay attention? We don't have to be Holy-rollers but if we changed the way we treated each other, do you think maybe it would be a great start.

> *"Everything is based on mind, is led by mind, is fashioned by mind. If you speak and act with a polluted mind, suffering will follow you, as the wheels of the oxcart follow the footsteps of the ox. Everything is based on mind, is led by mind, is fashioned by mind. If you speak and act with a pure mind, happiness will follow you, as a shadow clings to a form." –*
> *From Buddhism*

## Chapter Fifty one

# One's Grief

Every person has to grieve in their own way. No matter what you grieve for, it is a loss. You can not erase a person; their name won't disappear, the harder you fight it the closer they remain in your heart. There is no set time to grief, true friends will sit and listen no matter how many times you tell your story or mention the person's name. You can start off negative and beat yourself up or take a positive outlook and rejoice in all the happy memories that kept you together. We always forget the bad we minimalism these occurrences, the good will move to the forefront and joy will reign supreme.

Once we reach out and grasp our grief and take it in our heart it is then we begin to heal. It is the little things that stay, a simple statement, an expression we catch our self using that will bring back a memory. The worse we chose to punish someone and if it really wasn't warranted, the longer we will grieve. It is a way of cleansing our self and purifying the heart to move on.

Is disappointment one of our biggest grief's? The feeling that we never said something we should have. Something we left undone. No matter what the level of disappointment it is something that starts with in us and we have to deal with it before we can heal effectively. Qualities such as kindness, compassion and forgiveness are the seeds we want to plant. Unfortunately the self-centered ego's for grasping, gaining and selfishness easily covers them so deep we have trouble bringing them back to the surface. Once we get beyond the source of our grief and eliminate our woe-is-me ego's will our heart open to let new growth begin.

When we live in a level of grief, we constantly circle the rim of Pandora's Box every evil has the ability to rear its ugly head at any given time. The self control we bestow on the event is the only salvation we have to keep us from faltering away off our destined path in life. To have to detour and correct our previous mistakes could take several valuable years from our life. This is time that could have been spent in another level of spiritual realization through an open heart and a quality love for your own salvation.

Where I do so much family research through genealogy, I have on occasion gone to a cemetery to find a headstone to verify a fact or merely add a picture to my data base. I find these strolls through a cemetery very interesting. One can come up with so many questions that if the time was spent would offer up such stories. You can see such elaborate headstones you wonder if that was someone special or the guilt of one left behind showing its presence. There are some headstones you would like to research to see what the actual story was. Others like one I recently seen "Here Lies A True Friend" no date, do name nothing. What is that story?

You can see whole families marked in one area. Then one can see a mother in one spot and her spouse in an entirely different area. What was behind all that? These are areas where the mind shouldn't be in control. Take the extra step and view it from an open heart, understand the meaning. View it with love in your heart. Plant a seed that there was something good there. Maybe this was a person who died with no other family around to say these people should have been buried side by side. Or maybe this was a situation where one died very young and only a single plot was purchased. There are so many positive reasons that can be entertained rather than bad.

We went to Salem Massachusetts, because there was evidence a person in the family tree was tried as a witch. To my astonishment I found there were actually two people in the tree that were tried. To witness all these years later, the horrors these people were put through, makes one wonder how little we have advanced all these years later. We may not hang people as witches any more but we sure are guilty of prejudging and condemning others in our own minds for next to no reason. There was one action that stood out in mine and also in my son's mind. This older man was tried for a false reason just because he had a choice piece of land that other's wanted. He refused to offer up a plea of guilty or not so. He was tortured by covering him with a board and piling rocks on top. He never uttered a plea, but died in the process, his land remained in his family for hundreds of years after. It enhances the knowledge than we possess the ability to withstand anything if our will is strong enough.

After my initial separation and I decided to identify whether the problem was of my doing that caused this travesty. I took a course on raising children after separation and divorce. Through this course it was detailed the problems children experience at different developmental stages of their lives. Each age group had different titles and behaviour patterns. Where this to me is a level of grief experienced by all ages I would like to share some of that information. We all know people that we deal with on a day to day basis and if we can relate we can deal with it.

*Eyes Closed, Too Hear*

0-2 years -"The age of helplessness"
- Difficulty sleeping, eating or toileting
- Delays in learning skills
- Clinging, fear of separation from parent
- Crying, irritability, temper tantrums

2-4 years- "The age of guilt"
- Fantasizing about parents reconciling
- Anxiety at bedtime, sleep problems
- Fear of being abandoned by one or both parents
- Emotional neediness and clinging
- Whining, crying, aggression, tantrums
- Regression – a return to security blankets, baby talk, lapses in toilet training

5-8 years- "The age of sadness"
- General sadness, feeling abandoned and rejected
- Crying and sobbing
- Magical thinking
- Loyalty conflicts
- Longing for the absent parent
- Depression, sense of helplessness
- Regression

9-12 years-"The age of anger"
- Intense anger and increased aggression
- Blaming the parent they feel caused the divorce
- Feelings of loneliness
- Physical complaints, headaches and stomachaches
- Over activity to avoid thinking about the separation/divorce

- Shame about what is happening in the family
- Depression and suicidal fantasies
- Attempts to "take care of" the parent they perceive as most hurt

13-18 years- "The age of false maturity"
- Anger, avoidance, withdrawal, sadness, shame
- Depression, changes in sleep, grief over loss of family
- Anxiety over intimate relationships
- Becoming distant and aloof from family
- Feeling hurried to achieve independence
- Acting out emotional distress through sex, drugs, crime
- Fatigue, difficulty concentrating

Adult Children- "The age of dual roles"
- Shock – they may not have realized there were problems
- Anger – based on how they found out
- Grief – loss of the ideal – family traditions, childhood home, grandparent roles
- Shame/embarrassment – relating to new parental behaviours/ freedoms/ partners
- Identification – fear that their own relationship may fail

With this there are a multitude of do's and don'ts, I have expressed many throughout my book. If I were to dwell on any it would be the don'ts because they are so critical to affecting the ability to have an open heart and the true expression of loving one's self.

Don't
- Tell children more than they can grasp

- Allow children to become your "confidantes"
- Let children become part of the fight
- Say unkind things of other parent
- Have children spy
- Try to buy affection
- Compete for child's love
- Involve children with new partner too early
- Make comparison between child and former spouse
- Hesitate to seek professional help

<u>The most important fact is</u>: The child(ren) didn't cause this problem

In the book, *Dating for Dummies* [For Dummies, 1997], Dr. Joy Browne advises people to wait one full year after the divorce is final to start dating, with no exceptions.

Dr. Joy Browne does make good points about dating while married:

- "If you're married, don't date." A person should wait until their divorce is final before dating.
- "Who needs to date someone who is…capable of adultery or bad judgment or both?" A person should not date a person who is married.

Seeds that have been planted in us all our lives if we have had any type of upbringing at all. These values have quite often been overlooked in today's society where blended families are more the norm than anything else. Some don't know from one day to the next whose socks they are really wearing. Then you have to wonder about the possible social diseases that come with this open love lifestyle.

Today there is no excuse for saying; you didn't know what the end consequences might be. I have been separated coming on a year now, loneliness is my greatest nemesis. I have filled this time with writing my book, setting up a website and an extensive social media support for my website. I will know when the time is right to take another person in my life. Once I know that I have done everything in my power to ensure that the problems that ended my last relationship were either corrected, addressed or weren't mind to own.

I shall step forward proud in the knowledge that my heart is open to accept another person without prejudice of mind over nonexistent faults. I will have taken every corrective action possible and achieved the forgiveness in my own mind to proceed to my ultimate destiny.

I know now for me to sit and wait alone anticipating a possible phone call once a week is not how I want to live the rest of my life. To be alone, killing time, is not for me. There are only just so many things you can do to fill a day. I now can say I have paid my penance I have served my time; I achieved what I set out to do. The next steps are mine, I can walk away holding my head high knowing what I have learned has put me in fantastic standing to finish walking my destined path.

> *"That which is false troubles the heart, but truth brings joyous tranquility"* --- *Rumi*

## Chapter Fifty two

# Share Your Story

So many people keep their problems to themselves. These problems become festering wounds that if not exposed never really heal. This doesn't mean you have to go out and tell the whole world your problems, dreams and history to start. But it does mean you should find a non-bias person to relate your situation to and from there you expand your level of trust to include people as you see fit.

Amazing as it may seem once said out loud and being true a sense of relief will follow. If you can't say it out loud write it down, read it and throw it away. Keep doing this until it becomes second nature, you are now on your way to acceptance. I found by writing this book, my acceptance to my situations, has become real and profound. As I have said if I can help one person to modify their life, to open their heart and plant their seeds my purpose in life has taken on a real meaning.

If I can look into a person's eyes and relate to their feelings I feel I have removed some of their life pains. To hold a hand and relate helps heal the scars. Each story told, opens the mind to a situation experienced by the reader, it is then and only then that you can share your life story. Once the heart is open and the precious power is felt, the strength of healing will erase all the negative feelings and pains held within.

If you knew that one of your life stories could help a person get through their problems would you tell it? That is the question that goes through my mind in every chapter that I have written in this book. There are a lot of stories that have presented themselves but they don't really cover what I am trying to express.

The only story that fits to some degree is one where I spent a considerable amount of time with a co-worker after his wife had passed away. We spent hours walking through their life together it is hard to express the multitude of roller coaster emotions that were experienced. He slowly came out of his funk and started to live his life again. I have walked this mile a couple times now and must admit it never gets easier. People that deal with this day in day out have to harden to a certain degree but they have to feel it more when it becomes one of their own. All these different circumstances have to accumulate over a period of time. There are cases where people deal with problems that span a lifetime. The feelings have to literally blow the mind.

To express your thoughts in word is something that not everyone cares to do. Some people say you make it sound so easy. I will assure you this has been building for sixty years; I knew it was something I wanted to do but to bare ones soul to anyone that wants to take the time to read my story has to also be a yearning that they must fulfill also. To express a story than opens another is astounding. Just to think that our mind works in such a manner that we can relate to a similar situation and experience a whole new concept. Something that could have been left by the wayside so many years ago and it springs back like yesterday. No loss of time, until we really think about it. Then a smile graces our lips, and the heart feels a whole new feeling. That is the heart opening to accept the joy left behind. Another seed planted to re-live life's memories.

I was talking with my oldest sister and she said remember when dad was dying and the minister came over. I said yes and then she mentioned how some people found comfort by following the native customs by burning sweet grass. She stated it helped to remove any negative energy in the house. Yeah and we had to collect the buds off the female cedar bushes, a flat rock and a feather also. So we talked about that for awhile and remarked how that again was a different approach but very remarkable in its own right.

My one brother in law is native and his mother had a dream about a horse drawn carriage with a rider-less pony following behind. She felt something was about to happen and wanted to warn us. Later that day there was the reddest sunset one could image, as we looked out the window a horse drawn carriage with a rider-less pony went by. If you think that didn't cause a ruminating effect throughout the house that night. My brother in law definitely moved throughout the house burning sweet grass that night. That was our introduction to native culture first hand.

We are a very multi cultured family so to see the different customs and cultures come into play didn't shock us. We allowed everyone to follow their own lead to move beyond their own personal grief. Were we successful I would say from any outsider's point of view yes. But some four years later there remains a small level of doubt in some minds. To me some pain really never leaves, even though the bad memories do disappear. It takes a callused person to say they carry absolutely no grief over a loved one. That feeling can only be dealt with later in their own life. A seed of compassion planted for the one who grieves.

> *"What we have done for ourselves alone dies with us; what we have done for others and the world remains and is immortal."*
>
> *~ Albert Pike*

## Chapter Fifty three

# Too Heal

There is no set period of time for one's grief. Whereby, we all grieve in a different way. One thing for certain you can't erase a person's total existence or can they be totally eliminated from our lives. The harder we try the stronger the feelings get. A person has to talk things over to release their emotions whether it's with friends or family. The more we vent the sooner the healing process starts. Some people take months before the pain actually sets in.

*Grief is a tidal wave that over takes you,*
*smashes down upon you with unimaginable force,*
*sweeps you up into its darkness,*
*where you tumble and crash against*
*unidentifiable surfaces,*
*only to be thrown out on an unknown*
*beach, bruised, reshaped...*
*Grief will make a new person out of you,*
*if it doesn't kill you in the making.*
*Stephanie Ericsson*

As we go through our levels of healing, one may find comfort in an evidence for an afterlife. Some people look to psychic mediums who claim to communicate with spirits, individuals who believe they had a near-death experience, hypnotic regression for one who declares a method for past-life travel, and individuals who believe to have experienced an after-death communication from a loved one in spirit.

I truly believe a person will not start to heal until they look within and deal with their emotions from the inside out. Every outside influence merely introduces another hurdle to jump over in the end. Each hurdle carries its own scars and each scar has to heal at its own rate. The key to this whole situation is to be positive and work at everything with an open heart.

Once we get beyond the emotional baggage that clouds our inner feelings and slowly leave this baggage behind, will a person begin to heal? Emotional baggage once recognized is sorted from good to bad. We slowly forget the bad and only the good parts of our past remain, from this the open heart can heal. Our memories are so complex, we can remember the darndest stuff so minute in nature but also so memorable. It takes a power stronger than the mind to bend perception, override emotional circuitry, a power that can only come from the heart.

My mother likes to go to the cemetery and talk to my dad. There is a bench in front of their headstone; if she has a problem she needs to discuss she sits there and talks to him. Having been together for sixty years there is a level of comfort, a level of trust a general feeling of wellbeing by sharing her inner thoughts. The feeling I can only dream of, for I will never see sixty years with a companion, a confidant, a partner even if I lived to be a hundred and twenty plus. It isn't in the cards I nearly made two twenty fives but not sixty. It takes a rare few that can brag that existence. That longevity, to have seen every combination of happiness, stress, hurt and joy any person could imagine. She always returns from their private spot with a new glow and a different perspective on how to address her situation. She says dad gave me an answer. It is never complex, very logical, an answer that she can live with and moves on. The power of strong influences and yet another seed planted to an open heart.

It is like writing this book, the hardest thing to do is to express your thoughts in words so that a feeling is also expressed. A person can read a statement and argue a whole different meaning than what has been expressed. As in the written word we can write it, read it, go back and change it until we feel we have said exactly what we want to express. Then take the same situation and we express our thought out loud the same words are spewed out there for the analogs of time, they can't be effectively pulled back, chewed up and spit out again. We need to appreciate the feelings tried to be expressed when given from the heart. I stated once before in this book I say this because I love you to hear it from me only establishes the level of my sincerity. For you to hear something from a closed heart has a whole different meaning, it comes from judgement and a definite bias. These words once spoken take a long time to heal. Trust me, I have felt them more than once in my life and I can relate.

> *"Forgiveness is not always easy. At times, it feels more painful than the wound we suffered, to forgive the one that inflicted it. And yet, there is no peace without forgiveness."*
> 
>                                                    - Marianne Williamson

> *"Turn your wounds into wisdom"*
>                                                    --- Oprah Winfrey

## Chapter Fifty four

# Then Sings My Soul

I have always loved the sound of thunder, the flash of lightning, the power of the rumble through the heavens above. The louder the better, the stronger the flash, the nearby sizzle, what power! I am captivated, totally entranced. Nothing seems to reach into my inner being like a good thunder storm. My second wife and I used to love to sit and watch these heavenly splendours and marvel at the veracity of its splendour. My first wife would take my kids and put their rubber boots on and hide in the stairwell. What a difference between minds. Thus with every thunder storm, my mind goes to this hymn always has, always will.

*Eyes Closed, Too Hear*

## Then Sings My Soul

O Lord my God! when I in awesome wonder
Consider all the worlds Thy hands have made,
I see the stars, I hear the rolling thunder,
Thy power throughout the universe displayed:
Then sings my soul, my Savior God, to Thee:
How great Thou art, how great Thou art!
Then sings my soul! my Savior God, to Thee:
How great Thou art, how great Thou art!
When through the woods and forest glades I wander
And hear the birds sing sweetly in the trees;
When I look down from lofty mountain grandeur
And hear the brook and feel the gentle breeze:
Then sings my soul, my Savior God, to Thee:
How great Thou art, how great Thou art!
Then sings my soul! my Savior God, to Thee:
How great Thou art, how great Thou art!
And when I think that God, His Son not sparing,
Sent Him to die, I scarce can take it in;
That on the cross, my burden gladly bearing,
He bled and died to take away my sin:
Then sings my soul, my Savior God, to Thee:
How great Thou art, how great Thou art!
Then sings my soul! my Savior God, to Thee:
How great Thou art, how great Thou art!

> *When Christ shall come with shout of acclamation*
> *And take me home, what joy shall fill my heart!*
> *Then I shall bow in humble adoration,*
> *And there proclaim, my God, how great Thou art!*
> *Then sings my soul, my Savior God, to Thee:*
> *How great Thou art, how great Thou art!*
> *Then sings my soul! my Savior God, to Thee:*
> *How great Thou art, how great Thou art!*
> *Originally a Swedish folk melody,*
> *"O Store Gud" by Carl Boberg (1859-1940)*
> *was translated by Stuart K. Hine in 1899.*
> *sung by George Beverly "Bev" Shea.*

"How Great Thou Art" is a Christian hymn based on a Swedish poem written by Carl Gustav Boberg (1859–1940) in Sweden in 1885. The melody is a Swedish folk song. It was translated into English by British missionary Stuart K. Hine, who also added two original verses of his own composition. It was popularized by George Beverly Shea and Cliff Barrows during Billy Graham crusades.

Words can go no further than the feelings expressed in this hymn; once heard sung, a person has to keep it with them, somewhere close to their heart or they just aren't alive. My heart moves with this hymn at it always has. One really has to wonder how a hymn such as this can transcend language and travel the entire world through time. I remember the first time I sang it as an altar boy and I am still inspired to sing it in my mind at the more sensitive times of my life. Totally remarkable, a seed which

I encourage anyone to take a listen, it can be found on the internet.

> *"When you choose to become more, you are choosing to go on the greatest adventure of your life. We are taught that need something or SOMEONE outside ourselves to be happy. This is the greatest misunderstanding of our time. Seek all you want, eventually you will find that everything and anything you are looking for is within you. Become you own soul mate, partner in crime and best friend. When you do, you will attract all that and more into your life."*
> —*Author unknown*

> *"All religions are founded on the fear of the many and the cleverness of the few"*
> --- *Stendhal*

## Chapter Fifty five

# A Gift

Any gift a person can pass on is the gift of love from an open heart. With a heart that through all adversities will be there to carry you to a safer place in your life. Having said that and now realizing that asking for forgiveness for the way I may have treated people gives me the reassurance that I am constantly working to better myself. As I previously stated if I can pass this on to others I will feel I have been successful in my life. I didn't have to buy their love as so many feel they have to do today. The price tag has no bearing on this gift, matter a fact, it is priceless. If you have to ask what it means to the other, again the power of the gift is lost. It is the feeling and the feeling alone of giving yourself unconditionally to another that offers the greatest reward. This you can take with you, the seed is planted, your reward.

To look into a child's eyes and say I am doing this because I love you more than what money can buy is from the heart. To say "No" is not always bad, that makes you a parent looking out for their best interests. To buy their love to cover your inadequacies or guilt only adds to the hurts that will manifest later. Pass your gift of an open heart consistently and the rewards of joy will be forthcoming on a daily basis.

This is not an excuse to not have to buy anything, rather putting a limit to a situation where one tries to outdo the other. A gift does not have to be monetary; to be appreciated is all I am trying to say. On the same token, when referring to the opposite parent one should never use the statement "Your mother" or "Your father" that statement immediately puts a child on the other parent's side. It is human nature, we go into the defensive mode, just by mere words and children seek that common ground very quickly. As soon as we use the word "Your" we have introduced a separation in the family structure and a child feels it right away. There is nothing more pure than a child's mind if they feel there is a problem in the family structure; they will assume the blame is theirs before forming any other opinion. They will side with the parent they fear most until they find their comfort zone.

I believe this is the gift we are born with; it was free programming that comes with no induced influences. Only time and many adversities change this gift. Some may never feel these feelings through their whole life and others live them every day. If we carry so much emotional baggage that we can't see the true gift that we carry, then we must make changes. There is no other way to express this.

Our gift to the world is ourselves, once we master the thought that we are here for a purpose to pass our gift to someone else through the power of an open heart. We start the foundation where life can survive the foundation of our soul that allows future seeds to flourish. When we try to live life without this we generate a following of mutants with no morals, no direction not even solid ground to stand on. Spewing out vile comments, to make themselves look important, we see it every day. Once we recognize this, feeling sorry for their actions isn't enough? The need to take corrective action sets in that is the gift of an open heart. Nothing is more rewarding when you know you have helped a person re-evaluate their destined path.

*No kind action ever stops with itself. One kind action leads to another. Good example is followed. A single act of kindness throws out roots in all directions, and the roots spring up and make new trees. The greatest work that kindness does to others is that it makes them kind themselves.*
*~ Amelia Earhart*

*"In the present circumstances, no one can afford to assume that someone else will solve their problems. Each one of us has a responsibility to help guide our global family in the right direction. Good wishes are not sufficient; we must become actively engaged."*
*~ Dalai Lama*

## Chapter Fifty six

# My Angels

I believe we all have a guardian angel; it appears before us in true times of need. The frequency has a direct bearing on our level of belief. If we profess to be non-believers, we only feel this presence when we truly hit rock bottom. This is when we are most vulnerable and open to receive a possible visualization and set us on a new path.

As I previously stated I believe where so many situations have influenced my life that I have an angel that is very close to me at all times. I am being guided to an ultimate outcome of which I haven't seen the absolute conclusion. I know I am getting closer to where I must be or do but I also know I haven't achieved the ultimate knowledge to fulfill this calling either.

There are a multitude of questions asked on this subject. Questions like. Do guardian angels exist? Do they come to help and comfort humans in need? Why do they appear before and help some people and not others? Do I really have a guardian angel?

Studies carried out indicate over 65% of the population believe they have a personal guardian angel. There is no scientific evidence for angels, of course. The only "evidence" we have for their existence is the long religious tradition, stories from the Bible and the many anecdotes from people who believe these spiritual beings have affected their lives.

Ultimately, angels are most often a matter of faith, and many believers have offered their opinions on what a guardian angel's role can be in a person's life.

Having said all this I truly believe we are all influenced by a supporting power. There are far too many circumstances that the outcome should have been different. I was renovating this house one time by myself, there was a lot of bull work involved and with this had ended up with quite a bruise on one arm. I was under stress and feeling very panicky, just not feeling right. Off to the hospital I went and as I walked through the doors, someone asked if I was OK and I said "Help" as my knees began to buckle a wheelchair was pushed under me. It turned out I was having a heart attack. I was rushed by ambulance to a nearby major city, on route they had to stop once to revive me. After a series of tests and scans, it was concluded that a blood clot had passed through my heart doing a small bit of damage in its lower portion. I believe to this day that I was guided by a special hand to the hospital and into hands that took quick action to help me. I knew my time wasn't up but the experiences were too real to overlook also.

It is said if you want an answer from your guardian angel, one has to ask a clear concise question. If it is done in jest so will be the response in jest. If one asks in greed, the response will not be recognized. As stated throughout this book if a person with a sincere and open heart talks to their hidden support system goodness will follow. The respond may not be noticed immediately but there will be a positive result that will be recognized by the humbled recipient. Then if the situation warrants immediate action, that will be recognized also.

Not all situations can be addressed by a guardian angel; there is a bigger picture that has to be considered also. If we are destined to serve on this earth for only a short period of time to pass off a lesson or message and then move on. That will happen also, we have no guarantee other than what is placed before us. What we do with it, is ours and ours alone. Do it easy or do it hard the end result will be the same.

I have driven across our country at times when neither man nor beast should be out playing. I can only say it is at these times someone has to be sitting on my shoulders guiding me. I have walked down the centreline in a blizzard as my uncle drove behind to take my oldest son to see a doctor because he had ear infection so bad. To try lasting one more night would have absolutely cruel and undo torture.

I would like to think we all try to make sacrifices during our lives. We take chances to help others. This I have done on numerous occasions. I have driven through snow storms especially that for nothing but the grace of the heavens above I have made it through. I know we all have situations we can relate to when it comes to adverse weather. You hear of golfers getting struck with lightning on the golf course and by some miracle just walks away.

I am a Saturday child governed under the protecting wings of the silver angel for Saturday. We have been given many qualities to that command leadership and compassion for everyone around us. We long to help and comfort those in need. My qualities are further influenced by the angel of August that extends very similar direction.

> *"Don't ever save anything for a special occasion. Being alive is the special occasion."*
> *~Author Unknown~*

## Chapter Fifty seven

# Repent

"Everybody needs to repent. Whenever we hurt someone else, or we ourselves are hurt by our own actions, whenever we break a law, whenever we tell a lie, whenever we steal someone else's property or name, whenever we smear some other person's reputation we need to repent, because repentance means a change of mind, a change of attitude."

As I first started down the road after the gut wrenching day, being told your marriage was over. I went through a series of feelings, none good by no means; I wished a level of revenge upon this person I was with for sixteen years. Then I realized, I had to make sure within myself that I had done everything in my power to me being the person I was meant to be. One thought that kept coming to mind was "The reason you got into this condition where you let this kind of a matter go un-judged in your midst was because you forgot who you were." This statement to me is so true I had become a person, moulded in a mind of another person, a sort of concubine, a slave to a never satisfying condition. I asked for forgiveness and such a weight has been removed from me. I had made a new beginning.

I love them too much to hurt them. You do not love somebody by not telling them the truth. We often let people go on and on because we say we love them too much to hurt them. Stop, Look at that statement again, I do not know anything more self-deceptive than that statement. It may be true that we do not want to hurt someone, but do you know who that someone is? It is us. Bottom-line, we do not want to hurt ourselves. We know that if we say these things to this individual they are going to get angry at us and that will hurt us and that is what we are avoiding. When you love somebody and tell them the truth in a loving, affirmative way, you enable them to see that you really love them. If you are willing to risk this friendship in order to tell them the truth, you really do love them.

To repent comes in many forms; basically we are asking forgiveness for an action. To realize you have made this mistake is the initial step to admission, but the asking for forgiveness has to complete the transaction because that is what makes it ours. We can ask that others' hearts be open to receive this glory, but it is not ours to seek forgiveness for their actions.

How many lies have to be told before we have to own up and tell the truth? To repent to ourselves for being so insecure in our lives that we have to lie about everything that is happening within us. Once we can learn to be honest with ourselves the rest falls right into place. When we repent and seek forgiveness only then do we start to heal and look at things in a different light. If we lie to ourselves, it will come back again to rear its ugly head until it is dealt with effectively.

Swallow your pride you are only hurting yourself. A seed planted, left to flourish in the warmth of truth.

## Chapter Fifty eight

# In the Garden

This tune makes me feel so light and alive every time I hear it. The words move me to the point where my hair tingles on the back of my neck. I can't express it in words and that for me is something. I have felt this feeling ever since I was an altar boy in our local church growing up. The first time I heard to the last time I heard it the results are always the same. I feel very special and as one with this tune.

*Eyes Closed, Too Hear*

## In The Garden

*I come to the garden alone
While the dew is still on the roses
And the voice I hear falling on my ear
The Son of God discloses.*

*Refrain*

*And He walks with me, and He talks with me,
And He tells me I am His own;
And the joy we share as we tarry there,
None other has ever known.*

*He speaks, and the sound of His voice,
Is so sweet the birds hush their singing,
And the melody that He gave to me
Within my heart is ringing.*

*Refrain*

*I'd stay in the garden with Him
Though the night around me be falling,
But He bids me go; through the voice of woe
His voice to me is calling.*

*Refrain*


*Words: Charles Austin Miles (1912)*

"I read…the story of the greatest morn in history: "The first day of the week cometh Mary Magdalene early, while it was yet very dark, unto the sepulchre." Instantly, completely, there unfolded in my mind the scenes of the garden of Joseph….Out of the mists of the garden comes a form, halting, hesitating, tearful, seeking, turning from side to side in bewildering amazement. Faltering, bearing grief in every accent, with tear-dimmed eyes, she whispers, "If thou hast borne him hence"… "He speaks, and the sound of His voice is so sweet the birds hush their singing." Jesus said to her, "Mary!" Just one word from his lips, and forgot ten the heart aches, the long dreary hours….all the past blotted out in the presence of the Living Present and the Eternal Future."

Every person has their own favourite tunes and songs. Each holding their own memories, our minds take us back to an instance that where the song played a key part in our lives. I have so many that I can relate to and each one has its own memory. Really next time you hear a tune that you like shut your eyes as you listen to it and see where your mind flashes back to. I find it is quite fun and it is a real good experience to bring back old memories. One can do the same with old movies our minds hold a treasure house of locked in memories.

That is why when I say never think for one minute that you can erase your past without dealing with it. It will come and haunt you, one day out of the clear blue the weirdest thing happens you slid into a funk and low a behold what comes back but the problems you have never dealt with. The harder we try to hide something the stronger it comes back to bite. Deal with it. There is no set time frame; the irony is before we leave this earth you will have to deal with your actions. Open your heart and seek forgiveness, save yourself a lot of undo pain. Work at this all your life and treat people the way you would like to be treated. Simple.

That to me is where my walk in the garden has taken me. I had the opportunity to deal with the error of my ways and worked towards forgiveness. If I have missed someone and they ever have an opportunity to read this book I pray they consider my intent was there to express this thought to them. Missing them was not intentional rather the opportunity never presented itself. If I have ever made a promise I never kept the same thought applies. That is my seed I would like to pass in this chapter from my walk in the garden. Please forgive me. Now it is your turn, look deep into your heart and think of whom you may have wronged and deal with it.

## Chapter Fifty nine

# Amazing Grace

It is absolutely amazing how often the music to this hymn is used. I have seen it associated with several videos on You Tube and every time I hear the music it sends shivers down my spine. This is one reason why it hits the top three selections for my own departure from this earth. Not many actually know the words to this hymn, so at this point I would like to share.

*Eyes Closed, Too Hear*

## Amazing Grace

*Amazing Grace, how sweet the sound,
That saved a wretch like me -
I once was lost but now am found,
Was blind, but now, I see.*

*T'was Grace that taught -
my heart to fear.
And Grace, my fears relieved.
How precious did that Grace appear -
the hour I first believed.*

*Through many dangers, toils and snares -
we have already come.
T'was Grace that brought us safe thus far -
and Grace will lead us home.*

*The Lord has promised good to me -
His word my hope secures.
He will my shield and portion be -
as long as life endures.*

*When we've been here ten thousand years -
bright shining as the sun.
We've no less days to sing God's praise -
then when we've first begun.*

*Amazing Grace, how sweet the sound,
That saved a wretch like me -
I once was lost but now am found,
Was blind, but now, I see.*

Written by English poet and clergyman John Newton (1725–1807) published in 1779.

Newton wrote the words from personal experience. He grew up without any particular religious conviction but his life's path was formed by a variety of twists and coincidences that were often put into motion by his recalcitrant insubordination. He was pressed into the Royal Navy and became a sailor, eventually participating in the slave trade. One night a terrible storm battered his vessel so severely that he became frightened enough to call out to God for mercy, a moment that marked the beginning of his spiritual conversion. His career in slave trading lasted a few years more until he quit going to sea altogether and began studying theology.

## Chapter Sixty

# Real Deal

How many times have we heard this term this is the "Real Deal" is it a way to make something more authentic? There are countless ways this term seems to fit into our lives. What I have experienced how my life has taken a direction or a drawing to completely change how I deal with things to me is the real deal. To have visualization or a complete snapshot on what needs to happen in my life has to have meaning. To be compelled to write a book and a share a sense of direction has to have a meaning. Do I have the right to call this the real deal? The experience getting me to this point qualifies.

I am not hurting anyone rather pointing out facts, that if allowed to manifest in their own experiences could bring a simplified approach to inner peace. By opening the heart and loving yourself first puts a whole different feeling on your approach to life which does make it a real deal. By asking your maker for guidance, direction and forgiveness gives you a feeling that once felt will convince you it is the real deal.

I am not telling everyone to run out and put a bible under their pillow. To read at a moment's notice, this will not work. I am saying one should be aware of the moral issues that affect mankind and treat people the way they would like to be treated. I am saying to eliminate greed from your life and allow your heart to guide you. To know the wrongs you have done in your life will come back to haunt you when you least expect it. These to me are the real deal. Our inner purpose to be here on earth was not by chance a mistake. We are here for a reason, a purpose, to pass on our seeds for future generations.

There is a reason why such a small percentage of the world's population controls the largest percentage of its wealth. This is not meant to be a controlling factor in our lives. On the same token, why when some people have so much do we still see world poverty? One of these starving children may hold the key in their mind that will change mankind forever. The key that if lost may take generations to re-appear in someone else. There is no rule that says you have to be rich to have great thoughts. We have seen that of late. Why are so many big celebrities faltering? Maybe these pains have to be felt before this knowledge is stimulated to offer solutions.

We are not privy to the master plan, but I do believe it is not complicated. Life is what we make it not the other way around. We are the real deal; we were given the ability to think from the very beginning. Not saying we are using this ability to our best.

There is no doubt our world is quickly changing. The turmoil we are witnessing is a product of our own doing, we are in an evolution and I think the sooner we start dealing with the world's problems as a common governing body the better. Not the UN or the G20 but as a unified world governing body with one monetary system each country being responsible to supply its contribution to the common pot. There is so much duplication from county to county, state to state, province to province, country to country. We can no longer keep up to the infra structure required to maintain these duplications. Everyone wants to be the one in control, but I believe this is where the mistake begins. World powers are starting to recognize this you see this with the European Union and the North American Union. This real deal has to go away further right down to the bare basics and a rebuild. Our changing weather patterns, global warming and depletion of resources will further reinforce this need. This is going to have to happen sooner than we think. When does the world debit become so enormous that it has to be cancelled out or revamped? Whether it takes another world war to incite this or just a world disaster the time of this evolution is fast approaching. We will be forced to re-affirm our beliefs and or establish new ones but this change is close at hand. The seeds planted here have to replace a whole rain forest, multitudes of wetlands and natural forests. We have wasted our abundant resources to the point where we have exceeded our requirements by half. What this means we need an earth and a half to survive at the rate we are currently going. Something has to give and it will.

The real deal is when you look into your young child's eyes and say sorry but this is what we have left you. Make the best of it and oh by the way try to explain this to your children. Good Luck with that, now that is the real deal.

If and when we got to the point of a common currency the biggest hurdles to cross would be in what language it would be and "who would we trust" etched on it. This is a situation where the heart definitely has to be open and love of humanity top priority.

> *"A "NO" uttered from deepest conviction is better and greater than a "YES" merely uttered to please, or what is worse, to avoid trouble."*
>
> -Mahatma Gandhi

## Chapter Sixty one

# Mysteries

There are so many things that happen in one's life that are an absolute mystery. People stop and say I cannot for the life of me figure out why this has happened or that has happened. Then they will top it off by saying "That is a complete mystery".

We have situation and things that happen that are an absolute mystery. Why do some people survive a crash where the vehicle is absolutely destroyed and another person bumps their head and they die? Why does a person show up at an accident scene help everyone out and then disappear never to be seen again? Or a person acquires a super strength to lift a heavy object off another person. Then you hear of situations where an animal or pet sensing danger helps a person to safety.

I believe these are all happening around us at any given time. It is the person that questions such an incident that really brings it to others attention. Life itself is full of mysteries, a person pinned between two vehicles lives long enough to pass on a message to a loved one. Or one person survives a plane crash where everyone else dies. Why just that person lives? These questions are endless. The stories that compliment them are just as marvellous.

So, what is our real purpose in life? It can be summed up in one word "Survival". The human race in general has been around for generations, no mystery. The main thought behind each generation is too survive. Period. How we do it is an absolutely different thing. We can do it the righteous way or take advantage of every situation presented to us. If we take advantage of everything and everybody, this trait continues through each following generation until it has nowhere to go but be corrected. I believe what we are seeing today, is just that, so many things have gotten so far out of hand that a correction is taking place. Our world will realign and we will all be better off for it.

    I am not saying that this realignment is going to be easy, drastic times call for drastic measures. If floods and complete lose has to happen it will and the survivors will continue on to better our world. If our world requires a purge, I don't want to be the last one here to turn out the lights rather I would like to think I was heading in the right direction to guide my fellowman to some enlightened reward. If the righteous and pure of heart are meant to continue on then I feel expressing these thoughts in writing is merely a start to what has to happen. Life's mysteries will bring survival; our ultimate destiny has yet to be achieved.

    Where I have experienced so many déjà vu experiences, I often feel we are living in a universe that has a complete clone in another universe where these situations have already been experienced. Our spirit has the ability to shuttle between these worlds, and this is where the déjà vu action takes place. That we are living the same life in another realm following different paths so that we can become the most perfect person in our maker's image. It is a continuous cycle to a final perfection. Otherwise what purpose would disease and poverty truly serve? These people are doing a cleansing for past sins and will come back to complete their transformation into a perfectly rounded being. To me that thought is better than coming back as an insect to be crushed in a blink of an eye. To live a life cycle in a day, what can you possibly learn from that. Our purpose is bigger and greater that to me is life's mystery.

We are all one in the eyes of our maker. If we started from two beings and one was formed from the rib of the original man. Then what is so hard to imagine that the mystery of life cannot be something as simple as the pureness achieved from a open loving heart. Our soul forms the foundation to our maker's teachings.

If anyone queries why I use the term maker instead of say God it is for the sake of the reader. This way anyone reading this book can't really say "Oh this doesn't pertain to me, because it is beyond my beliefs". This is just another form of being politically correct. That is what to our society has demanded so that we don't offend anyone, or is it? We are merely justifying our own inadequate misgivings. Period. Another seed planted.

> *"Self-pity is our worst enemy and if we yield to it, we can never do anything wise in this world."*
>
> *- Helen Keller*

## Chapter Sixty two

# I Love You

I Love You, was the hardest statement for me to say for a good portion of my life. I would walk around the conversation to avoid using these words. Like I have said throughout this book I never felt my purpose in life. I was constantly looking for my direction. There was a point early in my second marriage, where I started to say these words. Slowly I got to accept these words in my conversation. I started to say "I Love You" after relapsing into one of rock bottom experiences, not realizing at the time. I was on the cusp of starting to feel a direction. At this point it wasn't strong like it is today. It was merely a warm feeling that happened every now and then.

When my second marriage came crashing to an end I felt abandoned. Cast into a sea of doubt, left to flounder by myself. I now realize if I never sought knowledge and seen that glimmer of light at the end of the tunnel. My life had the potential of being lost in bitterness, with no value for anybody. To walk into an empty room with something exciting to say and find no one there to share with, how quickly the tone changes. The meaning to aspire to something greater is stifled because there is no one to share it with. I wouldn't wish that on anybody, not even someone that deserves no better. To know that feeling, should never happen too many times in one's lifetime, for me once was too much. Why do we do it to each other? Like leaving something unsaid something as simple as "I'm sorry" has lingered on a good many tongues after something unforeseen happens to a love one. Is that what you want left to tarnish your memories if something happens?

The value of love showed its powers and I now have only pity for the person that has hurt me. A pity that they can have for what they do to others. I know that when I say "I Love You" it now comes from my heart and I will take it always with me. If mankind can change to accept one another, what a great place this could be.

I have witnessed through my dad's second oldest brother what rock bottom could do. He took his life when he lost all his money on a new business. He was newly married to his second wife, they were expecting a child. Through this act of selfishness a child that never had the opportunity to know his father. What a loss. A mother had to raise a child without a husband at a time when there was no socially accepted support. If there was a seed planted I pray it never grows. To have this come in another generation. I really hope not. I pray my seed that I plant will replace this defective one. The generations from here on can aspire to redeem themselves through an open heart. Swallowing their pride and correcting their actions. Free them self from their own personal prison.

We have all witnessed and or lived through a time where someone near and dear has chosen to shorten their life here on earth. What has to pass through the mind at that particular moment in time? The realization that this is the only alternative left. To go out in the backyard and blow your brains out or sit in a car and let the fumes take us away. What has to push a person to that point? I can see if it is a result of a major life threatening illness. We are so obsessed with moral issues that euthanasia is a problem that can't be logically dealt with. The unfortunate part is the person more than not takes someone else with them. And that to me is a sin beyond all sins. A greed that has to be only dealt with by our maker, this has to be beyond judgement by mankind. What secrets do we hold that are that profound? That to open the heart and face them is beyond question. To look within and demand what are we doing wrong? To not be able to say "I LOVE YOU" to even yourself, just the once.

> *"Wisdom is the right use of knowledge. To know is not to be wise. Many men know a great deal, and are all the greater fools for it. There is no fool so great a fool as a knowing fool. But to know how to use knowledge is to have wisdom."*
>
> *- Charles Spurgeon*

> *"We really have to understand the person we want to love. If our love is only a will to possess, it is not love. If we only think of ourselves, if we know only our own needs and ignore the needs of the other person, we cannot love"*
>
> *--- Thich Nhat Hanh*

## Chapter Sixty three

# The Seed

This is where I am going to cut off my book everything else will have to fall in between. A chapter for every year of my life with nothing actually relates to a specific length of time. It is merely a point that I have chosen. Through the expression of planting a seed it symbolizes a space of true learning in which your real Self can emerge and rise to its full brilliance in Soul, Mind and Body. Life is right now and it is only in the consciousness to love, that we find true and lasting peace and solace. The seed we pass on is the knowledge gained by so many generations before us. So that the world will be a better place, we really don't need history repeating itself time and time again.

## The Seed

*A slap on the face, a scowl,*
*A look of utter hate.*
*You wonder why me,*
*You feel like removing this person*
*From your family's tree.*
*No one wants to forget,*
*This terrible feeling felt.*
*The empty prison created here,*
*The destruction of a life.*
*or*
*A warm hand on the cheek, a smile,*
*A gaze of pure Love.*
*An open heart, the sun shining above*
*A seed is planted from this love*
*For the upcoming generations*
*A message from above.*
*The choice is only yours*
*How do you want to be remembered,*
*The seeds of freedom you planted here.*
*They are your creation.*

> "Everything you see has its roots in the unseen world. The forms may change, yet the essence remains the same. Every wonderful sight will vanish. Every sweet word will fade, The source

*they come from is eternal, growing, branching out, giving new life and new joy. The source is within you. And this whole world is springing up from it"*

*--- Rumi*

*My Question for today... Have I done today what God has asked me to do?*

*"Stop being so impressed with what other people are doing and get impressed about yourself. You have a story that the world wants to hear. Go tell it!"*

*- Stone Evans*

*I was born in Swan River Manitoba and raised in Kamsack Saskatchewan. I left home at seventeen and spent twenty six years in the Canadian military. My life has taken me through such a series of diverse events that the desire to share the stories that touched my life became a life goal. I believe everyone has a story to share and from each story another can be told. We relate to life events from experiences related by others. This book has no real beginning or end it is a mere snapshot in time. I purposely wrote this book using no names so others could relate to stories within their own life. We all have had people that impacted our lives and at that time there stories have moved us. Once gone they are not forgotten but some of their unique stories are. Read, enjoy, share.*